Domain-Sensitive Temporal Tagging

Synthesis Lectures on Human Language Technologies

Editor

Graeme Hirst, *University of Toronto*

Synthesis Lectures on Human Language Technologies is edited by Graeme Hirst of the University of Toronto. The series consists of 50- to 150-page monographs on topics relating to natural language processing, computational linguistics, information retrieval, and spoken language understanding. Emphasis is on important new techniques, on new applications, and on topics that combine two or more HLT subfields.

Domain-Sensitive Temporal Tagging
Jannik Strötgen and Michael Gertz
2016

Linked Lexical Knowledge Bases: Foundations and Applications
Iryna Gurevych, Judith Eckle-Kohler, and Michael Matuschek
2016

Bayesian Analysis in Natural Language Processing
Shay Cohen
2016

Metaphor: A Computational Perspective
Tony Veale, Ekaterina Shutova, and Beata Beigman Klebanov
2016

Grammatical Inference for Computational Linguistics
Jeffrey Heinz, Colin de la Higuera, and Menno van Zaanen
2015

Automatic Detection of Verbal Deception
Eileen Fitzpatrick, Joan Bachenko, and Tommaso Fornaciari
2015

Natural Language Processing for Social Media
Atefeh Farzindar and Diana Inkpen
2015

Introduction to Chinese Natural Language Processing
Kam-Fai Wong, Wenjie Li, Ruifeng Xu, and Zheng-sheng Zhang
2009

Introduction to Linguistic Annotation and Text Analytics
Graham Wilcock
2009

Dependency Parsing
Sandra Kübler, Ryan McDonald, and Joakim Nivre
2009

Statistical Language Models for Information Retrieval
ChengXiang Zhai
2008

Domain-Sensitive Temporal Tagging

Jannik Strötgen and Michael Gertz

ISBN: 978-3-031-01035-4   paperback
ISBN: 978-3-031-02163-3   ebook

DOI 10.1007/978-3-031-02163-3

A Publication in the Springer series
SYNTHESIS LECTURES ON HUMAN LANGUAGE TECHNOLOGIES

Lecture #36
Series Editor: Graeme Hirst, *University of Toronto*
Series ISSN
Print 1947-4040   Electronic 1947-4059

Domain-Sensitive Temporal Tagging

Jannik Strötgen
Max Planck Institute for Informatics, Saarbrücken, Germany

Michael Gertz
Heidelberg University, Germany

SYNTHESIS LECTURES ON HUMAN LANGUAGE TECHNOLOGIES #36

ABSTRACT

This book covers the topic of temporal tagging, the detection of temporal expressions and the normalization of their semantics to some standard format. It places a special focus on the challenges and opportunities of domain-sensitive temporal tagging. After providing background knowledge on the concept of time, the book continues with a comprehensive survey of current research on temporal tagging. The authors provide an overview of existing techniques and tools, and highlight key issues that need to be addressed. This book is a valuable resource for researchers and application developers who need to become familiar with the topic and want to know the recent trends, current tools and techniques, as well as different application domains in which temporal information is of utmost importance.

Due to the prevalence of temporal expressions in diverse types of documents and the importance of temporal information in any information space, temporal tagging is an important task in natural language processing (NLP), and applications of several domains can benefit from the output of temporal taggers to provide more meaningful and useful results.

In recent years, temporal tagging has been an active field in NLP and computational linguistics. Several approaches to temporal tagging have been proposed, annotation standards have been developed, gold standard data sets have been created, and research competitions have been organized. Furthermore, some temporal taggers have also been made publicly available so that temporal tagging output is not just exploited in research, but is finding its way into real world applications. In addition, this book particularly focuses on domain-specific temporal tagging of documents. This is a crucial aspect as different types of documents (e.g., news articles, narratives, and colloquial texts) result in diverse challenges for temporal taggers and should be processed in a domain-sensitive manner.

KEYWORDS

temporal tagging, temporal expressions, temporal annotation, time, time extraction, time recognition, time normalization, temporal information, domain sensitivity, cross-domain temporal tagging, domain-sensitive temporal tagging, information extraction, temporal information extraction, TIMEX3, TimeML, HeidelTime, timelines

Contents

List of Figures

List of Tables

Preface

Time matters! Whatever document we read, be it a news article, biography, some microblog, or a patient's record, to name but a few examples, temporal information embedded in the documents typically helps us determine the course of events and actions, to correlate events, and eventually to get an overview of the documents' content. Driven by the continuously increasing amount of textual data that is available on the Web, in electronic archives, and Intranet document repositories the computer-supported analysis and exploration of textual data has become a necessity and also a challenge in numerous application domains. Named Entity Recognition (NER), that is, the task of information extraction that aims at detecting and classifying elements in some text into predefined classes, such as locations, persons, organizations, and temporal expressions, has become a cornerstone of tools and techniques that help to address this challenge.

Only in the past two decades has the topic of temporal tagging as a specific type of NER task become a major focus in research and development. Temporal tagging addresses the extraction, classification, and normalization of temporal expressions that occur in text documents, and it is the prerequisite for temporal information extraction. By now, the important role of temporal tagging has been well recognized in application domains such as text summarization, question answering, information retrieval, and topic detection and tracking. In these applications of temporal tagging, results can be as simple as the fully automated construction of a timeline of events detected in a document's content and can be as complex as revealing the temporal discourse structure in documents.

To date, there is no book that provides a comprehensive overview of the various methods, tools, evaluation competitions, and challenges the tasks of temporal tagging are faced with in the presence of diverse types of textual data and application domains. This book aims at closing this gap. Starting from the very fundamental role and concepts of time in documents, it provides an up-to-date overview of annotation standards, techniques, and competitions for evaluating the quality of temporal taggers, annotated corpora (including non-English texts) used for evaluations and developments, as well as a detailed overview of temporal taggers.

As the title indicates, this book focuses particularly on temporal tagging of documents from different domains, including text data different from the well-studied domain of news articles. For this, we discuss the challenges and approaches temporal taggers have to consider when processing news-style, narrative-style, colloquial-style, and so-called autonomic-style documents, the latter covering documents that contain many temporal expressions that cannot be normalized to real points in time, but only according to some local or autonomic time frame. Examples of autonomic-style documents are specific types of scientific texts and literary works.

We believe that this book provides researchers, practitioners, and developers a valuable resource for designing and improving temporal tagging techniques and tools, or just for applying them in a useful manner as part of more complex text analysis and exploration pipelines. While publicly available temporal taggers already provide sophisticated output for several application scenarios, there is still a lot of work in this area ahead of us. This book aims at providing a solid foundation on which such work can be built.

Jannik Strötgen and Michael Gertz
Saarbrücken, Germany and Heidelberg, Germany
July 2016

Acknowledgments

This book gives an in-depth overview of methods, tools, and techniques of temporal tagging in different domains. Based on the number of publications and evaluation competitions, the past few years clearly show that this field is taking on an enormous interest in the research community and industry. We thus would like to thank all researchers who actively contribute new ideas to this field, organize evaluation competitions, and provide temporal tagging tools and resources for other researchers and the public.

Although this book is about temporal tagging in general and not just about our temporal tagger HeidelTime, we want to take the opportunity to thank all contributors of HeidelTime for their great work and many users for helpful feedback to further improve the tool. We also would like to thank the many students at Heidelberg University who contributed in the form of student projects, and bachelor and master theses.

In particular, we thank Anne-Lyse Minard and Steven Bethard for their valuable reviews of the draft of this book. They put a lot of effort into the reviews and provided numerous valuable comments as well as suggestions to significantly improve the book. Finally, we want to thank the series editor Graeme Hirst for his great support and his instant replies to all our questions. It is time for a big thank you!

CHAPTER 1

Introduction

Temporal tagging is a specific task in natural language processing (NLP), in which temporal expressions are extracted from text documents and normalized to some standard format. Since temporal expressions are prevalent in many types of documents and because temporal information is an important dimension in any information space, applications of several domains can benefit from the output of temporal taggers.

This book covers the topic of temporal tagging and is structured as follows. In this chapter, we describe the task of temporal tagging, and then present some examples of NLP and NLP-related application scenarios in which temporal information can be exploited to provide more meaningful and useful results. In Chapter 2, we provide background knowledge and cover basic concepts related to temporal information. The foundations of temporal tagging are described in Chapter 3, and temporal tagging of different types of documents and thus domain-sensitive temporal tagging are explained in Chapter 4. An overview of existing techniques and tools for temporal tagging including our own system HeidelTime is provided in Chapter 5. Finally, future research directions are discussed in Chapter 6. However, to guarantee the correct understanding of two important terms frequently used in this book, we start with defining the concepts "temporal expression" and "value of a temporal expression".

- A *temporal expression* is either an expression referring to a date or time of any granularity (e.g., "March 11, 2007", "yesterday", "June 2016", "20th century", "9 pm"), an expression referring to a duration (e.g., "three years", "several months"), or an expression referring to the periodical aspect of an event (e.g., "every Monday", "twice a week").

- The *value (of a temporal expression)* covers the (most important) semantics of the temporal expression in a standard format, that is, the normalized information of the expression.

Examples of and more details about different types of temporal expressions and annotation standards for temporal expressions will be covered later in this book, but these definitions are crucial to understand the task of temporal tagging, which is defined and explained next.

1.1 THE TASK OF TEMPORAL TAGGING

Temporal tagging addresses the extraction, classification, and normalization of temporal expressions occurring in text documents. It is a prerequisite of the full task of temporal annotation (temporal information extraction), which concerns the detection and interpretation of temporal expressions, events, and temporal relations between events and between temporal expressions and events [Verhagen et al., 2009]. However, temporal tagging is not only valuable in the context of temporal information extraction, but also in many research areas and application scenarios as will be detailed in Section 1.2.

In general, temporal tagging can be considered as a specific type of named entity recognition and normalization. Although the three standard named entity types are person, organization, and location [Nadeau and Sekine, 2007], "the notion of named entity is commonly extended to include things that are not entities per se, but nevertheless have practical importance and do have characteristic signatures that signal their presence" [Jurafsky and Martin, 2008, p. 762]. Thus, further types of information are sometimes also covered under the named entity umbrella, for example, genes and proteins, numbers, and temporal expressions.

The classical tasks of named entity recognition (NER) tools are to identify the spans of named entities in texts and to classify the extracted named entities into pre-defined classes of entities. Thus, the normalization of entities to a unique identifier or some value in a standard format is only performed if the named entities' normalization—depending on the type of entity also referred to as disambiguation, linking, or resolution—is addressed, too. In contrast, a temporal tagger identifies the spans of temporal expressions in texts and normalizes the expressions according to some standard format. Depending on the annotation specifications, expressions are also sometimes classified according to their type, e.g., whether an expression is a date (e.g., May 3, 2009) or a duration (e.g., three days). However, this classification of temporal expressions can be considered as a part of the normalization process and thus, one can specify the two subtasks of temporal tagging as follows.

- *Extraction*: given a text, determine the spans of all temporal expressions.

- *Normalization*: given a text and a set of extracted temporal expressions, assign the temporal semantics to each expression in the form of normalized values in a standard format that adheres to some annotation specification.

Figure 1.1 illustrates the two tasks of a temporal tagger. Given a text document (left), determine the temporal expressions (middle), and assign a normalized value in a standard format to each identified temporal expression (right). In Chapter 3, we will give an overview of existing annotation standards for temporal expressions. These define what should be considered as a temporal expression and how temporal expressions are to be normalized. Before that, however, we will first outline some application scenarios in which temporal expressions can be exploited, and then have a closer look at the concept of time in Chapter 2.

1.2   APPLICATION EXAMPLES EXPLOITING TEMPORAL TAGGING

For well-known NLP tasks such as named entity recognition (NER), there are many motivating application scenarios described in the literature. In the following, to illustrate the utility of temporal tagging, we present some use cases, in which applications can easily exploit extracted and

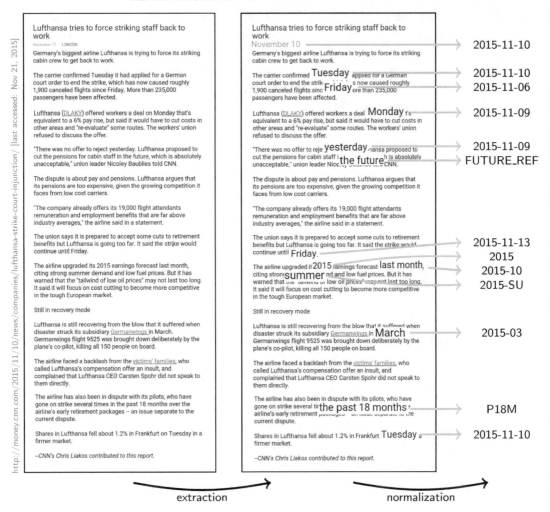

Figure 1.1: The two tasks of temporal tagging: extraction and normalization.

normalized temporal information and benefit from the output of temporal taggers and thus from the value of temporal information in general.

TEMPORAL TAGGING FOR INFORMATION EXTRACTION

In many text documents, *events* play an important role. Typically, events happen at some specific time and some specific place [Strötgen and Gertz, 2012a]. The importance of temporal information when organizing and summarizing extracted events is intuitive: given a text document with event mentions, the chronological ordering of the described events obviously benefits from normalized temporal expressions. Similar to temporal information, geographic information is also important in this context. However, the geographic aspect of events is out of the scope of this book.

As illustrated in Figure 1.2, many documents do not mention events in a chronological order. Typically, sections about specific topics are used and contain temporally overlapping content. Further examples are biographies that often contain temporally overlapping sections about, for instance, "private life" and "professional life", and news articles that report on recent happenings before referring to events that have happened in the past. An example of such a news article is shown in Figure 1.3.

Similar to the task of summarizing and ordering events extracted from documents, temporal fact extraction also requires temporal tagging output. For instance, when collecting facts for a knowledge base, it should be taken into account that most facts are not static but either evolve with time or are valid only during a particular time period [Kuzey and Weikum, 2012]. For instance, *"Bill Clinton"* holdsPoliticalPosition *"President of the United States"* is a correct fact but only valid for a specific time period.

While extracting events and temporal relations from single documents has a rather long tradition and was, for instance, addressed in the TempEval competitions at SemEval 2007 [Verhagen et al., 2007], 2010 [Verhagen et al., 2010], and 2013 [UzZaman et al., 2013], research was more recently extended to perform cross-document temporal relation extraction, as in the Timeline task of SemEval 2015 [Minard et al., 2015].[1] A further indication of the importance of temporal tagging in the context of information extraction is the fact that at the 2015 SemEval competition, in addition to the Timeline task, three additional shared tasks were organized, in which extracted and normalized temporal expressions are a prerequisite to successfully address the tasks: QA TempEval[2] [Llorens et al., 2015], Clinical TempEval[3] [Bethard et al., 2015], and Diachronic Text Evaluation[4] [Popescu and Strapparava, 2015].

TEMPORAL TAGGING FOR TOPIC DETECTION AND TRACKING

The goal of topic detection and tracking (TDT) is to organize news documents in an event-based way by building clusters of topics [Allan, 2002]. In this context, a topic is typically defined as "a seminal event or activity, along with all directly related events and activities" [Fiscus and Doddington, 2002]. For instance, the very first news article about a plane crash opens a new topic, and following news articles such as reports about the number of fatalities belong to the same topic. In contrast, news articles reporting about another plane crash do not belong to the same cluster. To decide whether an upcoming news document belongs to an existing cluster or opens a new cluster, the similarity between documents is typically determined based on some

---

[1]Timeline: Cross-Document Event Ordering, http://alt.qcri.org/semeval2015/task4/ [last accessed: Nov 9, 2015].
[2]Question Answering TempEval, http://alt.qcri.org/semeval2015/task5/ [last accessed: Nov 9, 2015].
[3]Clinical TempEval, http://alt.qcri.org/semeval2015/task6/ [last accessed: Nov 9, 2015].
[4]Diachronic Text Evaluation, http://alt.qcri.org/semeval2015/task7/ [last accessed: Nov 9, 2015].

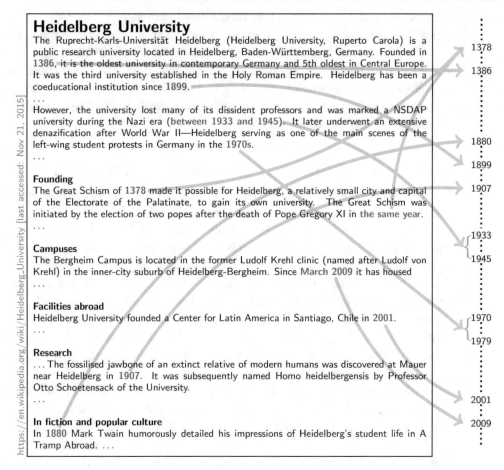

Heidelberg University

The Ruprecht-Karls-Universität Heidelberg (Heidelberg University, Ruperto Carola) is a public research university located in Heidelberg, Baden-Württemberg, Germany. Founded in 1386, it is the oldest university in contemporary Germany and 5th oldest in Central Europe. It was the third university established in the Holy Roman Empire. Heidelberg has been a coeducational institution since 1899.

...

However, the university lost many of its dissident professors and was marked a NSDAP university during the Nazi era (between 1933 and 1945). It later underwent an extensive denazification after World War II—Heidelberg serving as one of the main scenes of the left-wing student protests in Germany in the 1970s.

...

Founding

The Great Schism of 1378 made it possible for Heidelberg, a relatively small city and capital of the Electorate of the Palatinate, to gain its own university. The Great Schism was initiated by the election of two popes after the death of Pope Gregory XI in the same year.

...

Campuses

The Bergheim Campus is located in the former Ludolf Krehl clinic (named after Ludolf von Krehl) in the inner-city suburb of Heidelberg-Bergheim. Since March 2009 it has housed

...

Facilities abroad

Heidelberg University founded a Center for Latin America in Santiago, Chile in 2001.

...

Research

...The fossilised jawbone of an extinct relative of modern humans was discovered at Mauer near Heidelberg in 1907. It was subsequently named Homo heidelbergensis by Professor Otto Schoetensack of the University.

...

In fiction and popular culture

In 1880 Mark Twain humorously detailed his impressions of Heidelberg's student life in A Tramp Abroad. ...

https://en.wikipedia.org/wiki/Heidelberg_University [last accessed: Nov 21, 2015]

1378
1386
1880
1899
1907
1933
1945
1970
1979
2001
2009

Figure 1.2: Excerpts of the Wikipedia page about "Heidelberg University" and a timeline to which occurring temporal expressions are mapped. The content is not reported in a chronological order due to different topical sections about Heidelberg University. Thus, temporal tagging is crucial to correctly extract and order event information in a chronological way.

Lufthansa tries to force striking staff back to work November 10, 2015
The carrier confirmed Tuesday it had applied for a German court order to end the strike, which has now caused roughly 1,900 canceled flights since Friday.

...

Lufthansa is still recovering from the blow that it suffered when disaster struck its subsidiary Germanwings in March. ...

March 2015
November 6, 2015
November 10, 2015

http://money.cnn.com/2015/11/10/news/companies/lufthansa-strike-court-injunction [last accessed: Nov 21, 2015]

Figure 1.3: Excerpts of the CNNMoney article of Figure 1.1. After reporting on a recent happening, it refers to an event from the past in its last paragraph. Again temporal tagging is crucial to correctly extract and order event information.

information extracted from the documents. For instance, Makkonen et al. [2003] create event vectors consisting of (i) names, (ii) locations, (iii) temporals, and (iv) content words.

In general, ambiguous expressions—such as *"Tuesday"*, *"Friday"*, and *"March"* in the news article shown in Figure 1.3—are quite frequent in news documents. To be able to exploit information about temporal expressions occurring in documents, temporal tagging is again a prerequisite because not just the detection but in particular the normalization of temporal expressions is crucial for successful topic detection and tracking.

TEMPORAL TAGGING FOR INFORMATION RETRIEVAL

During recent years, the value of temporal information has been increasingly exploited in the context of information retrieval research and applications [Alonso et al., 2007, 2011, Campos et al., 2014, Derczynski et al., 2015, Kanhabua et al., 2015]. Note, however, that there are different types of temporal information that can be used in information retrieval scenarios. The two main aspects are (i) time as a dimension of relevance and (ii) time as query topic.

On the one hand, when time is used as a dimension of relevance, temporal tagging is not needed. However, information about the document creation time is typically utilized to improve the ranking of documents. For example, for news-related queries, the freshness of search results may be important [see, e.g., Li and Croft, 2003]. In addition to improving search results, time as contextual information can be used to perform time-sensitive query auto-completion [Sengstock and Gertz, 2011, Shokouhi and Radinsky, 2012].

On the other hand, temporal tagging plays a crucial role when time is a query topic. No matter whether the temporal part of a query is provided explicitly or implicitly, temporal expressions occurring in potentially relevant documents have to be detected, normalized, and compared to the temporal aspect of the query. Berberich et al. [2010], for instance, integrate temporal expressions into a language modeling approach, and Strötgen and Gertz [2012a] present a query model to explicitly formulate temporal queries in a flexible way. Note that time as query topic must be handled by search engines, because temporal queries occur frequently as was shown by some query log analyses of web search engines: Nunes et al. [2008] found 1.5% queries with explicit temporal information, Metzler et al. [2009] determined 7% queries with implicit temporal intent, and Zhang et al. [2010] reported 13.8% for queries with explicit time and 17.1% with implicit time.

Note that sometimes the document creation time of a document might be a good indicator for detecting whether a document is relevant for a given query. However, using a temporal tagger to analyze the documents' content is often crucial to successfully find relevant documents. For instance, both documents shown in Figure 1.4 can be considered as relevant for the example information need *"Germanwings"* with the time interval of interest being set to *"1st of March 2015 to 30th of April 2015"*. While the first document is a news document also published during the time interval of interest, the second document is a news article published in November 2015, that is, outside of the time interval of interest. However, both documents contain temporal expressions

March 25, 2015	November 10, 2015
Germanwings plane crash: Leaders visit Alps site	**Lufthansa tries to force striking staff back to work**
The German, French and Spanish leaders have arrived together in the French Alps to visit the scene where a Germanwings plane crashed on Tuesday, killing all 150 on board. ...	The carrier confirmed Tuesday it had applied for a German court order . . . Lufthansa is still recovering from the blow that it suffered when disaster struck its subsidiary Germanwings in March. . . .

left: http://www.bbc.com/news/world-europe-32046250 [last accessed: Nov 21, 2015]
right: http://money.cnn.com/2015/11/10/news/companies/lufthansa-strike-court-injunction [last accessed: Nov 21, 2015]

Figure 1.4: Temporal information retrieval example. Given the query (*"Germanwings"*, *"1st of March 2015 to 30th of April 2015"*), both documents can be identified as relevant if a temporal tagger is used to extract and normalize the temporal expressions in the documents' content.

referring to the Germanwings plane crash in March 2015 (*"Tuesday"* and *"March"*, respectively), and they thus satisfy the information need.

A further interesting observation from Figure 1.4 is that the term *"Tuesday"* in the first document refers to a date within the time interval of interest (March 24, 2015) while the same term in the second document does not (here, it refers to November 10, 2015).

TEMPORAL TAGGING FOR QUESTION ANSWERING

A further area in which time is a crucial dimension is question answering. While this is one commonality with information retrieval, the two tasks share further aspects: In both areas, a user is faced with an information need, and the goal of both information retrieval and question answering is to satisfy this information need. In contrast, the main differences between them is that in information retrieval, the information need is typically formulated as a query consisting of keywords—possibly enriched with time intervals of interest in the area of temporal information retrieval—but in question answering, the information need is formulated as a natural language question. Analogously, the presentation of results is also different: in information retrieval, a ranked list of relevant documents is typically presented to the user while in question answering, the answer to the information need is directly provided.

On the border between both areas lies so-called entity-oriented search [Balog et al., 2012]. A typical information retrieval query is to ask for a specific entity or fact about an entity. Thus, the goal of entity-oriented search is—as in question answering—to directly provide an answer, in the ideal case together with a justification, e.g., in the form of small text nuggets rather than full-length documents [Pasca, 2008]. An example of such a query with a temporal dimension is the query *"Golden Gate bridge built"* with the answer *"1937"*.

A research competition dealing with temporal (and geographic) information needs is NT-CIR GeoTime [Gey et al., 2010, 2011]. As in question answering, the information needs are formulated as natural language questions. Due to the temporal and geographic focus of the competition, the questions contain *"where"* and *"when"* aspects. However, unlike in standard question answering, systems are not evaluated based on whether they provide the correct answer, but on whether or not the documents ranked in a result list answer the question and are thus relevant. That is, the evaluation is performed in an information retrieval fashion.

In contrast to entity-oriented search and GeoTime, which both directly benefit from extracted and normalized temporal expressions, time-related question answering often deals with more complex temporal phenomena [Pustejovsky et al., 2005]. Then, temporal tagging on its own is not sufficient but temporal reasoning is often necessary, for example, to answer questions of the form *"did event x happen before event y?"*. To be able to automatically answer such questions, the full task of temporal information extraction is required—including the subtasks of temporal tagging, event extraction, and temporal relation extraction. In the recent QA TempEval challenge at SemEval 2015, in which temporal information extraction systems were to be developed, the systems were evaluated solely based on how well they perform in answering such time-related questions for which temporal reasoning is important [Llorens et al., 2015]. In Chapter 3, we will detail how temporal taggers can be evaluated in general.

TEMPORAL TAGGING FOR SUMMARIZATION

While the value of temporal tagging for the above examples is quite straightforward, there are further application scenarios, in which temporal tagging can provide more indirect benefits. An example of such an application scenario is the document summarization task.

In the text summarization community, it is well known that coreference resolution is valuable to create better text summaries [Azzam et al., 1999, Steinberger et al., 2007]. Similar to coreference relations between (proper) nouns and pronouns, the relations between temporal expressions could also be taken into account to improve summaries. Assume the document that is to be summarized contains the following two sentences consecutively:

- $s_1 = \langle$*In 2010, something unimportant happened.*$\rangle$

- $s_2 = \langle$*One year later, something important happened.*$\rangle$

Obviously, good document summarizations should contain important information, that is, in our example s_2 should be part of the summary but s_1 should not be contained in the summary. However, without proper context information, the semantics of s_2 is unclear due to the ambiguity of *"One year later"*. To fully understand s_2, the reader requires a reference time to resolve the relative temporal expression. Unfortunately, this reference time is part of s_1 (*"2010"*).

One solution to address this issue is to include both sentences in a summary. However, this results in a summary containing unimportant content, so that a better approach is to exploit the information provided by a temporal tagger (in s_2 that *"One year later"* refers to 2011). In this way, the unimportant sentence s_1 could be skipped, and s_2 could be part of the summary in a slightly modified way, for instance, starting with *"One year later (2011), something important happened"*. Note that even for the first solution, some information about occurring temporal expressions is necessary, namely that s_1 contains the reference time of s_2.

1.3   SUMMARY OF THE CHAPTER

In the context of temporal tagging, two tasks can be distinguished: extraction and normalization of temporal expressions. In several NLP-related research areas, and thus in many applications, temporal tagging output can be exploited to improve the approaches. Note that for almost all applications and research topics exploiting temporal information, the normalization subtask is highly crucial.

CHAPTER 2

The Concept of Time

In the previous chapter, we already have implicitly exploited some characteristics of temporal information to explain the motivating examples. Now, we formulate the key characteristics of temporal information in a precise manner (Section 2.1). Then, we highlight the differences between multiple types of temporal expressions occurring in textual documents (Section 2.2) and analyze their possible textual realizations (Section 2.3).

2.1   KEY CHARACTERISTICS OF TEMPORAL INFORMATION

There are three key characteristics of temporal information that make this kind of information highly valuable for many search and exploration tasks. They can be formulated as follows [Alonso et al., 2011].

TEMPORAL INFORMATION IS WELL DEFINED

Given two points in time or two time intervals, the temporal relationship between them can always be determined, for example, as before or identical. In general, the relationship can be assumed to be one of the temporal relations defined by Allen [1983] in the context of temporal reasoning. In addition to the equality relation, there are six symmetrical relations, namely before, meets, overlaps, during, starts, and finishes [Allen, 1983]. In Figure 2.1, these relations are visualized following Allen's presentation.

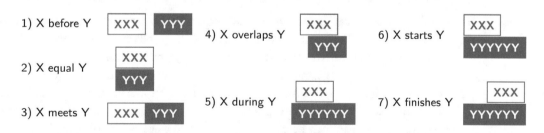

Figure 2.1: Temporal information is well-defined so that one of the relations defined by Allen [1983] holds between any intervals X and Y. Note that all relations except the equality relation are symmetric so that in total there are 13 possible relations between X and Y.

TEMPORAL INFORMATION CAN BE NORMALIZED

Regardless of the terms used and even of the languages used, two temporal expressions referring to the same semantics can be normalized to the same value in some standard format. Thus, temporal information can be considered as term- and language-independent. Understanding how temporal expressions can be normalized is one important step toward realizing how temporal information can be exploited in all kinds of application and research scenarios. While we will discuss the details when introducing annotation standards for temporal information in Section 3.1, an example with different temporal expressions carrying the same meaning is shown in Figure 2.2. Note that the expressions are uttered at various reference times (t_{ref}) and are normalized to the same value on the timeline t.

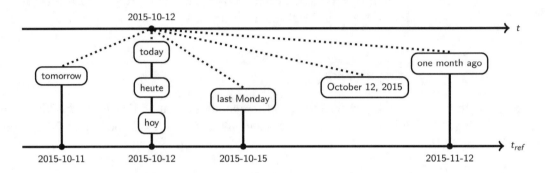

Figure 2.2: Temporal information can be normalized; the expressions uttered at various times t_{ref} have the same value in standard format (2015-10-12). Note that explicit expressions such as *"October 12, 2015"* are normalized independently of when they are stated. The terms *"heute"* and *"hoy"* are German and Spanish translations of *"today"*.

TEMPORAL INFORMATION CAN BE ORGANIZED HIERARCHICALLY

Temporal expressions can be of different granularities. For example, they can be of granularity day (e.g., *"August 3, 1992"*), month (e.g., *"August 1992"*), or year (e.g., *"1992"*). Due to the fact that years consist of months and months consist of days, expressions of one granularity (e.g., day) can be mapped to coarser granularities (e.g., month or year) based on the hierarchy of temporal information. In Figure 2.3, this hierarchy information is shown using the concept of timelines. A timeline is associated with a specific granularity (e.g., t_{day}, t_{month}, $t_{quarter}$, t_{year}) so that expressions of respective granularities can be placed on the timelines as points in time. Note, however, that coarse expressions represent a point on the timeline with the same granularity (e.g., "August 1992" on t_{month}) but span a time interval on finer granularities (e.g., "August 1992" spans from "August 1, 1992" to "August 31, 1992" on t_{day}).

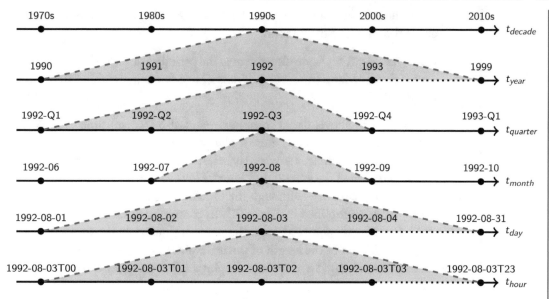

Figure 2.3: Temporal information can be organized hierarchically. The blue triangles show how points on coarser timelines (e.g., "1990s" on t_{decade}) span an interval on finer timelines (e.g., "1990s" spans from "1990" to "1999" on t_{year}).

2.2   TEMPORAL EXPRESSIONS IN DOCUMENTS

There are different types of temporal expressions according to what kind of temporal information an expression refers to, for example, a point in time or a duration. Note that we use the term *point in time* to refer to an expression if it can be anchored on a timeline of any granularity although, strictly speaking, expressions of coarse granularities span a time interval on finer granularities (cf. Figure 2.3).

In the context of temporal tagging, it is common practice to distinguish between the following four types of expressions—as it is specified in the temporal markup language TimeML, which will be detailed in Section 3.1 together with further annotation standards.

- *Date expressions:* A date expression refers to a point in time of the granularity "day" (e.g., *"July 10, 2015"*) or any other coarser granularity, for example, "month" (e.g., *"July 2015"*) or "year" (e.g., *"2015"*).

- *Time expressions:* A time expression refers to a point in time of any granularity smaller than "day" such as a part of a day (e.g., *"Friday morning"*) or time of a day (e.g., *"3:30 pm"*).

- *Duration expressions:* A duration expression provides information about the length of an interval. They can refer to intervals of different granularities (e.g., *"three hours"* or *"five years"*). In addition to the length of the interval, it might also be possible to specify the point in time when the interval starts or ends. However, the main semantics of a duration expression is about the length of the interval.

- *Set expressions:* A set expression refers to the periodical aspect of an event, that is, it describes a set of times or dates (e.g., *"every Monday"*) or a frequency within a time interval (e.g., *"twice a week"*).

As mentioned above, date expressions—and also (coarse) time expressions—can also be considered as time intervals since there is always a smaller temporal unit out of which such expressions consist, for example, a single "day" as a point in time consists of hours and could thus be regarded as a duration of the granularity "hour". However, time and date expressions can be placed on timelines as single points—although the timelines are of different granularities depending on the expressions, as exemplified in Figure 2.3. In contrast, a duration expression cannot be placed on a timeline as a single point although the point in time when the interval starts or ends might be specified in addition to the length of the interval. Thus, time and date expressions of different granularities are not treated as durations despite the fact that they often have a duration.

2.3   REALIZATIONS OF TEMPORAL EXPRESSIONS

Temporal expressions, in particular those of the types "date" and "time", can be realized in natural language in several different ways. Besides the fact that the full variety of realizations should be covered and thus extracted by a temporal tagger, a major issue is that depending on the realization, the difficulty in the normalization of date and time expressions varies significantly.

Many different terms have been used in the literature to describe various realizations and characteristics of point expressions, and a brief survey of alternative namings and their descriptions is given below. In this book, we use the four types of realizations described by Strötgen [2015], whose namings are motivated by observations earlier discussed in the literature. However, the goal of the four types is to cover those characteristics of point expressions that are particularly relevant for temporal tagging. In Table 2.1, the four categories are shown with sample expressions and an explanation of what information is required for their normalization.

- *Explicit expressions:* Explicit expressions are date and time expressions that carry all the required information for their normalization. Thus, no further knowledge or context information is required, the expressions are fully specified and context-independent. For example, the expressions of the granularity day *"March 11, 2013"* and of the granularity month *"March 2013"* can be directly normalized to 2013-03-11 and 2013-03, respectively.

- *Implicit expressions:* Implicit expressions can be normalized once their implicit temporal semantics is known. Thus, this category is designed specifically for named dates. Examples are holidays that can be directly mapped to a point in time. A simple implicit expression is *"Christmas 2013"* since Christmas refers to December 25. Thus, the expression can be normalized to 2013-12-25. A more complex example is *"Columbus Day 2013"* since Columbus

Table 2.1: The four categories how temporal expressions can be realized with examples and an overview of information required for their normalization

Category	Explicit	Implicit	Relative	Underspecified
Examples	May 4, 2011 October 1999	Columbus Day 2013 Christmas 2016	Today One year later	December Monday
Information required for normalization	None	Additional, non-standard temporal knowledge	Reference time	Reference time, relation to reference time

Day is scheduled as the second Monday in October. Some calendar calculations have to be performed to normalize the expression to 2013-10-14.

- *Relative expressions:* In contrast to explicit and implicit expressions, relative expressions cannot be normalized without context information. More precisely, a reference time has to be detected to normalize expressions such as *"today"* and *"the following year"*. For some relative expressions, the reference time is the point in time when the expression was formulated (e.g., for *"today"*) while the reference time of other expressions is a point in time mentioned in the context of the expression (e.g., in the statement *"in 2000 … in the following year"*, 2001 is the normalized value of *"the following year"* since *"2000"* is the reference time). In both cases, the reference time is the only required information, because the relation to the reference time is carried by the expressions.

- *Underspecified expressions:* For the normalization of underspecified expressions, the relation to the reference time is required in addition to the reference time itself. For instance, expressions such as *"December"* or *"December 25"* can locally be normalized to XXXX-12 and XXXX-12-25, respectively, that is, without specifying the year. Assuming that the reference time is "November 2013" (2013-11) and the relation to the reference time is "after", then the two examples can be normalized to 2013-12 and 2013-12-25, respectively.

ALTERNATIVE NAMINGS

As mentioned above, the categorization of temporal expressions referring to points in time has quite a long tradition in the literature. While the set of expressions which we call explicit expressions is usually a fixed set and only the names to refer to such expressions differ—e.g., explicit [e.g., Alonso et al., 2007, Schilder and Habel, 2001], fully specified [e.g., Pustejovsky et al., 2003a], absolute [e.g., Derczynski, 2013, Jurafsky and Martin, 2008], complete [e.g., Hinrichs, 1986], and independent [e.g., Hinrichs, 1986]—expressions we call implicit are less frequently discussed. Grouping the other expressions (i.e., the ones we refer to as relative and underspecified) results in different, partially overlapping sets with multiple names in the literature.

In the following, we present Mazur's [2012] overview of the terminology used in the literature. For this, the following three example expressions are used:

(i) *"tomorrow"*,

(ii) *"2 days later"*, and

(iii) *"May 21st"*.

While some authors summarize all three types of expressions, e.g., as indexical expressions [e.g., Schilder and Habel, 2001] or relative expressions [e.g., Alonso et al., 2007], they were already separated into three groups by Smith [1978] and Hinrichs [1986]. Expressions such as (i) are frequently referred to as deictic expressions [e.g., Ahn et al., 2005, Busemann et al., 1997, Hinrichs, 1986, Smith, 1978]. Expressions such as (ii) are referred to as anaphoric expressions by some authors [Busemann et al., 1997], while others use the same term to refer to expressions such as (ii) and (iii) [e.g., Ahn et al., 2005]. In our categorization, we follow Busemann et al. [1997] referring to expressions such as (iii) as underspecified expressions.

Some authors include so-called "vague expressions" as a separate group of point expressions. For instance, Mani and Wilson [2000b] use the term to refer to expressions such as *"Monday morning"* or season names (e.g., *"fall"*, *"winter"*) as vague expressions since their boundaries are fuzzy. That is, there are no exact start and end times. However, we agree with Mazur [2012] that the vagueness of such expressions should not result in a specific type of expressions since it "is not the expression that is vague [...] [but] the entity referred to that has vague boundaries" [Mazur, 2012].

UNCERTAINTY OF TEMPORAL EXPRESSIONS

Standard date and time expressions are also often used without referring to the full duration of the expression. That is, the actual meaning of them is uncertain, or more specifically, it is not clear which exact time interval they actually refer to [Berberich et al., 2010]. For instance, in *"he visited Germany in 2010"*, it is rather unlikely that the visit took place the whole year. The exact point or period in 2010 is not known. Thus, all expressions of a larger granularity than a timestamp could be regarded as fuzzy. As will be described in Chapter 3, according to annotation standards, date and time expressions are typically assigned a single normalized value so that we also refer to them as points in time (with specific granularities). However, as pointed out by Berberich et al. [2010]—and as we will also discuss later in Section 3.1 when describing annotation standards—for some applications it may be useful to consider every time and date expression as an interval and to assign lower and upper bounds for the start and end times instead of a single value, that is, to take care of the fuzziness issue.

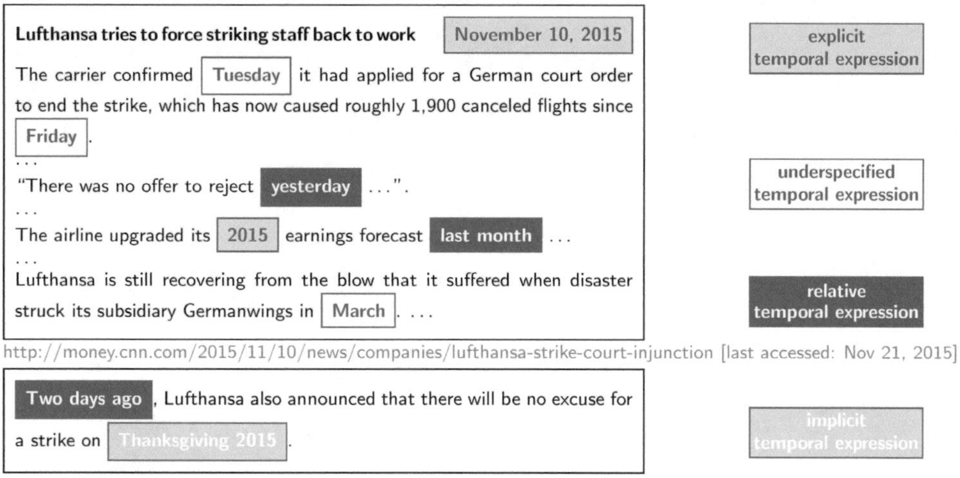

Figure 2.4: Different realization types of date expressions in documents.

EXAMPLES OF DATE EXPRESSIONS IN A NEWS ARTICLE

In order to become familiar with the naming of realization types of date and time expressions, we give some examples in Figure 2.4. In some excerpts of the news article, which was already shown in Figure 1.1, temporal expressions are marked as either explicit, underspecified, or relative. Since there has been no implicit temporal expression in the original article, we added the last sentence to the example to cover all four realization types of temporal expressions in this example.

As already pointed out above, there are differences in how temporal expressions of the four realization types are to be normalized. Since these differences are one of the key challenges of temporal tagging, we will cover them in detail in Chapter 4. Before that, we will first lay some further foundations (annotation standards and evaluation methods) and present an overview of relevant research competitions as well as existing annotated data sets in the next chapter.

2.4   SUMMARY OF THE CHAPTER

The most important characteristic of temporal information in the context of temporal tagging is that it can be normalized. For applications exploiting normalized temporal information, it is furthermore important that temporal information is well defined and that it can be organized hierarchically. While there are four types of temporal expressions (date, time, duration, and set expressions), several namings of the realizations of date and time expressions have been suggested in the literature. However, in the context of temporal tagging, we suggest to distinguish between explicit, implicit, relative, and underspecified date and time expressions.

CHAPTER 3

Foundations of Temporal Tagging

In this chapter, we lay the theoretical foundations to fully understand the discipline of temporal tagging and the challenges that approaches to temporal tagging are faced with. For this, we survey annotation standards, evaluation methods, research competitions, and temporally annotated corpora.

3.1 ANNOTATION STANDARDS

As introduced in the previous chapter, there are different types of temporal expressions: date, time, duration, and set expressions. In addition, temporal expressions can carry their meaning explicitly or implicitly, or they can be underspecified or relative to some context information. When addressing the task of temporal tagging, it is necessary that it is well defined: (i) what types of temporal expressions are "markable" [Ferro et al., 2005b] and should thus be annotated; (ii) what extents should be annotated; and (iii) how the semantics of the expressions can be captured by using normalization attributes requiring some values in a standard format. Thus, annotation standards with precise specifications are a prerequisite when dealing with the task of temporal tagging.

Currently, there are two widely used annotation standards for annotating temporal expressions in documents: TIDES TIMEX2 [Ferro et al., 2001, 2005b] and TimeML [Pustejovsky et al., 2003a, 2005, 2010], a specification language for temporal annotation using TIMEX3 tags for temporal expressions. Both standards present guidelines for the annotation of temporal expressions, including how to determine the extents of expressions and their normalizations. In both cases, the normalization is defined according to the ISO 8601 standard for temporal information with some extensions. For instance, a date expression of granularity day is normalized in the format YYYY-MM-DD. Since all widely used annotated corpora (cf. Section 3.4) as well as all state-of-the-art systems (cf. Chapter 5) are based on either one of the two above-mentioned standards, we describe the details of both of them in the following.

TIDES TIMEX2

While there have been several TIMEX definitions reaching from extent-only coverage [see, e.g., Chinchor, 1998], up to inclusion of some normalization information [see, e.g., Mani and Wilson, 2000a, Setzer and Gaizauskas, 2000], the TIDES TIMEX2 definitions were the first annotation guidelines that were well defined with sufficient detail to become broadly accepted as a standard. The annotation guidelines are based on the principles that temporal expressions should be tagged "if a human can determine a value for [it]" and that the value "must be based on evidence internal to the document" [Ferro et al., 2001]. Covering extent and normalization information, both questions *What is a temporal expression?* and *What is the meaning of a temporal expression?* are addressed. For the normalization, TIMEX2 tags may contain the following attributes [Ferro et al., 2005b]:

- *VAL:* a normalized form of the date/time [or duration/set];

- *MOD:* captures temporal modifiers;

- *ANCHOR_VAL:* a normalized form of an anchoring date/time [of a duration];

- *ANCHOR_DIR:* the relative direction between VAL and ANCHOR_VAL; and

- *SET:* identifies expressions denoting sets of times.

Except for the SET attribute, there is no concrete attribute for the type of temporal expressions in general. Nevertheless, since it can be determined based on the VAL attribute whether an expression is a time, a date or a duration, the classification of temporal expressions into these four types is implicitly covered by TIMEX2 annotations. However, it is rather difficult to use TIMEX2 annotations if only the extraction and classification of temporal expressions is targeted without the full normalization of temporal expressions.

TIMEML WITH TIMEX3 TAGS FOR TEMPORAL EXPRESSIONS

TimeML, which has more recently been formalized to create the ISO standard ISO-TimeML[1] [Pustejovsky et al., 2010], is based on the TIDES standard and was developed to capture further types of temporal information in documents. In contrast to TIDES that has only one tag for temporal expressions, TimeML contains tags for annotating events, temporal links (i.e., temporal relations), and temporal signals in addition to the TIMEX3 tag for temporal expressions [Pustejovsky et al., 2003a, 2005, 2010]. In the following, we focus on a description of TimeML aspects that are relevant for the task of temporal tagging.

Due to the fact that TimeML focuses on temporal information in general and not only temporal expressions, there are significant differences between TIMEX2 and TIMEX3. These differences concern both the attributes and the extents of temporal expressions. For example, events can be part of temporal expressions in TIMEX2 (`<TIMEX2>two days after the revolution</TIMEX2>`), while they are not part of temporal expressions following TimeML (`<TIMEX3>two days</TIMEX3> after the revolution`).

---

[1]ISO 24617-1: Language resource management—Semantic annotation framework (SemAF)—Part 1: Time and events (SemAF-Time, ISO-TimeML), `http://www.iso.org/iso/home/store/catalogue_tc/catalogue_detail.htm?c snumber=37331` [last accessed: May 15, 2016].

In particular, specific types of pre- and post-modifiers of temporal expressions are part of TIMEX2 tags while in TimeML they are outside TIMEX3 tags [Mazur, 2012]. Such constructs are handled using the newly introduced tags for annotating relations between temporal expressions and events. In addition, TIMEX3 tags cannot be nested. However, TIMEX3 tags with no extent are introduced, for example, to deal with unspecified time points, which are sometimes needed to anchor durations. Note that despite the fact that such abstract tags, that is, annotations without any extent, are described in the TimeML annotation guidelines, they have not been used [cf. Mazur, 2012]—neither in annotated corpora nor by TIMEX3-compliant temporal taggers—until the Italian temporal tagging challenge EVENTI in 2014 [Caselli et al., 2014]. In addition, abstract tags have been annotated in the 2016 released MEANTIME corpus [Minard et al., 2016], which was developed in the context of the NewsReader project.[2] Before that, empty TIMEX3 tags have been mostly ignored.

To describe the semantics of temporal expressions, the most important attributes of TIMEX3 tags[3] are:

- *type:* defines whether the expression is of type date, time, duration, or set;

- *value:* a normalized form of the expression;

- *mod:* captures temporal modifiers;

- *quant* and *freq:* specify the quantity and frequency of set expressions;

- *beginpoint* and *endpoint:* anchor begin and end of a duration; and

- *tid:* automatically assigned id number.

While the attribute *type*—with possible values "date", "time", "duration", and "set"—is newly introduced in TIMEX3, the attributes *value* and *mod* are similar to the VAL and MOD attributes in TIMEX2. These two attributes already capture a large part of the information of temporal expressions, and for many expressions—in particular for many date and time expressions—the *value* attribute is the only attribute besides *type* that is needed for normalization. This is also the reason why in several evaluations of temporal taggers, the *value* attribute is the focus of interest [see, e.g., UzZaman et al., 2013].

In particular for explicit date and time expressions, forming the *value* attribute (or the *VAL* attribute in TIMEX2) is straightforward, for example, the values of the expressions "*September 13, 2009*" and "*Oct 12, 2014 7:00 am*" are 2009-09-13 and 2014-10-12T07:00, respectively. For underspecified and relative date and time expressions, setting the value attribute is more challenging, because the information covered by their own extents is not sufficient. In contrast, a reference time has to be used along with a temporal function to calculate the content of the value attribute.

---

[2] http://www.newsreader-project.eu/ [last accessed: May 15, 2016].
[3] The details of the attributes are described in the TimeML annotation guidelines including further attributes, e.g., to capture the function of a temporal expression in a document. For details, see http://www.timeml.org/ [last accessed: Nov 3, 2015].

For instance, in a document published on November 27, 2014 (2014-11-27), the expression *"yesterday"* can be normalized to 2014-11-26.[4]

Value attributes in TIMEX3 (as *VAL* attributes in TIMEX2) assigned to duration expressions start with "P" (period), followed by an amount and an abbreviated unit, e.g., the value of *"three years"* is P3Y. If the unit of the duration is smaller than a day, the value attribute starts with "PT" (period, time), e.g., PT5H for the expression *"five hours"*. Thus, the value attribute of durations represents the length of the duration. If a duration can be anchored to some point in time, the attribute *beginpoint* or *endpoint* can be used to cover this information. Finally, the value attributes of set expressions are often similar to the ones of duration expressions. However, set expressions are additionally assigned at least one of the attributes *quant* and *freq* to cover the characteristics of set expressions. For instance, *"twice a week"*, has a value attribute of P1W and a freq attribute of 2X.

In contrast to the other attributes, the *tid* attribute does not contain any normalized information about an expression, but is just an id number that is automatically generated. It can be used to refer from other TimeML objects to a particular TIMEX3 object. Due to the relations between annotated instances within TimeML, for example, a temporal relation between an event and a temporal expression, an id is assigned to all objects in TimeML.

For many temporal expressions, only an identifier, a type, and a value are assigned. In addition, although the different attributes and definitions of extents between TIMEX2 and TIMEX3 are significant, the annotations for many temporal expressions are very similar, and an automated conversion works reasonably well [see Saquete, 2010, Saquete and Pustejovsky, 2011].

ANNOTATION SPECIFICATIONS FOR OTHER LANGUAGES THAN ENGLISH

While annotation standards have mostly focused on English or have been developed with the assumption of being rather language-independent, more recently, more and more effort was put into developing language-specific annotation specifications that capture language characteristics. Obviously, most of the language-specific adaptations deal with specifying extents of temporal expressions. For instance, TimeML specifies that determiners are typically included and prepositions are excluded of the extents of temporal expressions (e.g., in <TIMEX3>the year 2000</TIMEX3>). In other languages, however, contractions are sometimes used with prepositions and determiners (e.g., in German *"in dem"* can be contracted to *"im"* and thus the respective German phrase could be annotated either as <TIMEX3>im Jahr 2000</TIMEX3> or as im <TIMEX3>Jahr 2000</TIMEX3>). For this, there is a need for a decision whether to include both or neither of them in the extents of temporal expressions.

Furthermore, the set of possible normalization values for the temporal expressions' attributes have to be extended. For instance, while the original TimeML TIMEX3 attribute *value*

---

[4]Note that TimeML contains tags such as *temporalFunction* to document the usage of reference times and temporal functions, but since these are hardly used by any temporal taggers, we do not discuss them here. For details, we refer to Pustejovsky et al. [2005].

has a possible value to specify a quarter of a year using "Q", e.g., in 2015-Q1 and 2015-Q2 for the first and second quarter of the year 2015, respectively, it does not contain possible values to specify the three four-month periods of a year. While this is quite logical since references to quarters of years are frequent in English, references to the three four-month periods are not. However, when being faced with other languages, such expressions occur frequently. For instance, in Spanish the phrase <TIMEX3>el primer cuatrimestre</TIMEX3> refers to the first four-month period of a year. Obviously, it should be possible to normalize such expressions accordingly.

Language-specific annotation guidelines and specifications following the English TimeML have been developed for several languages. Often, they have been developed in the context of some research competitions or together with a manually annotated corpus, which will be surveyed in Section 3.3 and Section 3.4, respectively. These efforts resulted in annotation guidelines and specifications, with some of them being very sophisticated, e.g., those for French [Bittar et al., 2011], Spanish [Saurí and Badia, 2012a, Saurí et al., 2010], and Italian (Ita-TimeML) [Caselli, 2010, Caselli et al., 2011]. It is interesting to note that many of the adaptations to the guidelines and specifications do not concern the annotations of temporal expressions but other parts of TimeML.

For Portuguese [Costa and Branco, 2012] and Romanian [Forascu and Tufis, 2012], English TimeML-annotated data was translated and the annotations were aligned. The authors of both works report that modifications to the original TimeML annotations were sometimes necessary due to language differences, but mostly concerned events and temporal relations, that is, not temporal expression annotations. First steps toward TimeML-compliant annotation specifications for further languages have been taken without focusing on temporal expressions, e.g., for Turkish [Seker and Diri, 2010]. For some languages, annotation efforts concentrated on TIMEX3 annotations only, e.g., for Vietnamese and Arabic [Strötgen et al., 2014a], Croatian [Skukan et al., 2014] and Turkish [Küçük and Küçük, 2015]. These, however, did not result in language-specific annotation specifications but have been carried out by following the English annotation guidelines for TIMEX3 annotations as closely as possible.

HANDLING THE UNCERTAINTY OF TEMPORAL EXPRESSIONS

According to both standards, TIDES TIMEX2 and TimeML with TIMEX3 tags, temporal expressions referring to points on timelines of any granularity are associated with a single *value* attribute. For instance, <TIMEX>the year 2000</TIMEX>, <TIMEX>March 2000</TIMEX>, and <TIMEX>March 11, 2000</TIMEX> are normalized to 2000, 2000-03, and 2000-03-11, respectively. As pointed out by Berberich et al. [2010], such temporal expressions carry some amount of uncertainty if they occur in a specific context. For instance, in the phrase *"the FIFA world cup final 1998"*, the final took place on a particular day and not during the whole year.

Thus, they suggest handling each date and time expression as a four-tuple with lower bounds (l) and upper bounds (u) for the begin and end times to cover this uncertainty, i.e., as $\langle begin_l, begin_u, end_l, end_u \rangle$. For single temporal expressions the lower bounds are identical and the upper bounds are identical (e.g., the four-tuple representation of <TIMEX>May

2000</TIMEX> is ⟨2000-05-01, 2000-05-31, 2000-05-01, 2000-05-31⟩). For interval expressions, the four values are different, e.g., ⟨2000-03-01, 2000-03-31, 2001-05-01, 2001-05-31⟩ for <TIMEX>March 2000 to May 2001</TIMEX>.

When strictly following TimeML, the phrase *"March 2000 to May 2001"* is to be annotated as two date expressions (<TIMEX>March 2000</TIMEX> and <TIMEX>May 2001</TIMEX>) and a duration expression as abstract tag with the value attribute covering the length of the interval (1 year and 3 months). In addition, the begin and end of the interval are covered by the *beginpoint* and *endpoint* attributes normalized as 2000-03 and 2001-05. However, as pointed out above, these empty TIMEX tags are often ignored and thus the duration information about complex temporal expressions is typically not covered.

It is worth mentioning that such a crisp annotation of temporal expressions using the four-tuple representation is not always possible due to the fuzziness of language. For instance, temporal expressions with modifiers are more difficult to interpret. In such cases, TimeML makes use of the modifier attribute in addition to the value attribute, e.g., <TIMEX>the beginning of 2000</TIMEX> has a value attribute of 2000 and a modifier attribute of START. Thus, the annotation is left fuzzy on purpose. A direct resolution to the four-tuple representation is also difficult. Of course, due to the fuzziness one could assign the same four values as if there was no modifier. However, it is obvious that parts of the year are not part of "the beginning of 2000" and specifying the boundary is difficult, if not impossible. The boundary might also depend on when the expression is uttered. If the time of utterance is March 2000, then it is likely that March is not included in the time referred to as "the beginning of 2000". In contrast, March might be included if the expression is uttered in 2002. The upper bound of the end time can thus not be determined at all.

SUMMARY

TIDES TIMEX2 and TimeML annotation standards are widely accepted in the research community. Depending on particular use cases, they are sometimes extended—as by Berberich et al. [2010] in the context of temporal information retrieval—to better cover the requirements of applications. Due to a lot of research on temporal relation extraction, TimeML is more widely used than TIDES TIMEX2 annotations.

Whenever one is faced with the task of temporal tagging, annotation specifications are required so that normalized information can be correctly interpreted. In addition, since almost all works in the area of temporal tagging are following one of the two standards, it is crucial to follow these annotation specifications when developing a temporal tagger. Otherwise, existing manually annotated corpora cannot be used for evaluations and no meaningful comparison to existing approaches is possible.

Based on both standards, several research competitions have been organized, and several corpora have been manually annotated to be used as benchmarks. In the following sections, we survey temporal tagging research competitions and present an overview of existing annotated corpora. As different measures have been used in the research competitions to evaluate temporal tagging performance, we first describe how temporal taggers can be evaluated and what issues have to be taken into consideration.

3.2 EVALUATING TEMPORAL TAGGERS

In general, as for many natural language processing tasks, there are two ways of evaluating the extraction and normalization quality of temporal taggers: extrinsically and intrinsically. In the former case, more complex tasks or applications relying on temporal tagging output are evaluated. Examples are the tasks of temporal information retrieval [Alonso et al., 2011], temporal relation extraction [UzZaman et al., 2013], and (time-related) question answering [Llorens et al., 2015]. Much more common to evaluate temporal taggers, however, are intrinsic evaluations, that is, using manually annotated corpora and directly evaluating a temporal tagger's extraction and normalization quality.

CONFUSION MATRIX

For intrinsic evaluations, temporal tagging is considered as a specific sequential tagging task, and the confusion matrix (also called contingency table or contingency matrix) can be used to describe a system's output when compared to a gold standard. As shown in Table 3.1, all decisions of a temporal tagger can be grouped with the confusion matrix into one of the following four classes of a binary classification [Manning and Schütze, 2003]:

- true positives (TP): annotated by the system and in the gold standard;

- true negatives (TN): neither annotated by the system nor in the gold standard;

- false positives (FP): annotated by the system but not in the gold standard; and

- false negatives (FN): not annotated by the system but in the gold standard.

   Note that because many temporal expressions consist of more than one token, it is also common to distinguish between strict and relaxed matching. Details about the differences will be explained at the end of the section (page 29).

Table 3.1: The decisions of a temporal tagger can be categorized using the confusion matrix

System Prediction	Gold Standard (Ground Truth)	
	Positive	Negative
Positive	TP	FP
Negative	FN	TN

PRECISION, RECALL, F_1-SCORE

Both tasks of temporal taggers—the extraction and the normalization of temporal expressions—can be evaluated based on the confusion matrix. For the extraction, true positives are all instances that are correctly extracted by the system, while for the normalization, only instances that are correctly extracted and normalized are considered as true positives. Typically, in an evaluation the measures of precision, recall, and f_1-score are determined.

Precision is a measure to indicate how many of the expressions extracted by the system are correct (Equation 3.1). If all instances marked as positive by the system are correct, then precision equals 1, and if all instances marked as positive by the system are incorrectly marked, then precision equals 0:

$$precision = \frac{TP}{TP + FP}.$$ (3.1)

In contrast, recall indicates how many of the expressions that should be extracted are correctly extracted by the system (Equation 3.2). Thus, recall equals 0 if none of the instances that should be marked as positive is marked as positive by the system, and recall equals 1 if all instances that should be marked as positive are indeed marked as positive by the system:

$$recall = \frac{TP}{TP + FN}.$$ (3.2)

Obviously, there is a trade-off between precision and recall. Marking all instances as positive results in a recall of 1 while marking only a single instance correctly as positive results in a precision of 1. Depending on the ratio of positive and negative instances in the gold standard, the other measures would be rather low if these strategies were applied. That is, precision would be low if all instances were marked as positive, and recall would be low if only a single instance was marked as positive. Once a system already reaches a specific level for precision and recall, an increase of one of the measures usually involves a decrease of the other measure. Thus, the goal is often to find a good balance between precision and recall. To determine what "good" is, the f_β-score (also called f_β-measure) can be calculated (Equation 3.3). It measures the weighted harmonic mean of precision and recall:

$$f_\beta\text{-}score = \frac{(1 + \beta^2) \times precision \times recall}{\beta^2 \times precision + recall}.$$ (3.3)

Depending on the choice of β, precision and recall can be weighted differently. Frequently used values for β are 0.5, 1, and 2. The $f_{0.5}$-score weights the precision twice, and the f_2-score weights the recall twice. The most frequently used f_β-score is the f_1-score to calculate the balanced harmonic mean (Equation 3.4). It is often also referred to as f-score or f-measure:

$$f_1\text{-}score = \frac{2 \times precision \times recall}{precision + recall}.$$ (3.4)

EVALUATING THE EXTRACTION AND THE NORMALIZATION SUBTASKS

Note that in the context of temporal tagging, the measures precision, recall, and f-score can be calculated for the extraction subtask or for the full task of temporal tagging, that is, for the extraction and the normalization. In the first case, a temporal expression is considered as true positive (TP) if it is extracted by the system and marked in the gold standard. In the latter case, a temporal expression is only considered as true positive if it is extracted by the system and marked in the gold standard, and, if it is additionally normalized correctly.

Although temporal expressions may have multiple attributes containing normalization information as defined in the annotation standards discussed in Section 3.1, there is a tendency that the focus of the evaluation is put on the TIMEX3 attributes *type* and *value*, with the value attribute being considered as most important, e.g., in the TempEval-3 competition [UzZaman et al., 2013]. Instead of evaluating the normalization quality of temporal taggers based on the temporal expressions' *value* attribute, one could either calculate the evaluation measures considering the joint set of normalization attributes, or for each attribute independently.

NORMALIZATION ACCURACY

An alternative measure to precision, recall, and f-score, which is sometimes used to report the normalization quality of a temporal tagger, is accuracy. In general, the difference between precision and accuracy is that precision deals only with a system's decisions about the instances marked as positive in the gold standard, that is, only true positives (TP) and false positives (FP) are considered. In contrast, accuracy calculates the correctness of all decisions independent of whether instances are marked as positive or negative in the gold standard. Thus, accuracy is calculated as the ratio of correct decisions to all decisions:

$$\text{accuracy} = \frac{TP + TN}{TP + FP + TN + FN}. \tag{3.5}$$

Note that for the extraction of temporal expressions, accuracy (Equation 3.5) is usually not meaningful. Due to the sparsity of temporal expressions in text documents, the class of true negatives is typically huge, resulting in high accuracy values independent of how well temporal expressions are actually handled by the system. In contrast, the quality of the normalization subtask is sometimes reported using the so-called normalization-accuracy measure. Note that the set of all decisions then does not contain decisions about all temporal expressions but only about those extracted by the system (Equation 3.6). Normalization-accuracy indicates if the temporal expressions correctly extracted by the system are also normalized correctly:

$$\text{normalization-accuracy} = \frac{\text{correctly normalized expressions}}{\text{correctly extracted expressions}}. \tag{3.6}$$

In order to compare the overall quality of temporal taggers, the extraction and normalization quality of temporal taggers should be considered together. In addition, the normalization

Table 3.2: Evaluation example: on a corpus with 100 temporal expressions, the extraction and normal-ization quality of four fictitious systems is evaluated using precision, recall, f-score, and normalization-accuracy; for some measures, B outperforms A; similarly, either C outperforms D or vice versa although they have identical f_1-scores for the full task of temporal tagging

	System A	System B	System C	System D
TP Extracted/Normalized	1/1	100/99	75/60	53/52
FN Extracted/Normalized	99/99	0/1	25/40	47/48
FP Extracted/Normalized	0/0	1/1	20/20	4/4
Extraction Quality				
Precision	**1.00**	0.99	0.79	**0.93**
Recall	0.01	**1.00**	**0.75**	0.53
F-score	0.02	**0.99**	**0.77**	0.68
Extraction and Normalization Quality				
Precision	**1.00**	0.99	0.75	**0.93**
Recall	0.01	**0.99**	**0.60**	0.52
F-score	0.02	**0.99**	**0.67**	**0.67**
Normalization Quality				
Normalization-accuracy	**1.00**	0.99	0.80	**0.98**

quality of two systems with different recall values in the extraction task should not be directly compared based on the normalization-accuracy without considering the recall of the extraction. A system can achieve a higher accuracy score than another system although the latter normalizes more temporal expressions correctly.

EVALUATION EXAMPLE

In Table 3.2, we show some evaluation results of four fictitious systems to demonstrate the im-portance of reporting a temporal tagger's extraction and normalization performance in a concise manner to allow for meaningful comparisons. Assuming system A correctly extracts only one temporal expression and also normalizes it correctly. Furthermore, assuming system B correctly extracts all entities and correctly normalizes all extracted entities except of one. In addition, sys-tem B extracts a spurious temporal expression. Then, system B has lower precision values for the extraction and for the full task of temporal tagging than system A and also a lower normalization-accuracy.

In addition, we compare systems C and D, which achieve an identical f_1-score for the full task of temporal tagging. However, while system C is more balanced with respect to precision and recall, system D outperforms system C clearly with respect to precision and normalization-accuracy.

Depending on which of the evaluation measures are reported, different systems may be considered as performing better. Although reporting all measures would allow for a most complete comparison, often only some of the measures are reported. For instance, in the TempEval-2 competition [Verhagen et al., 2010], precision, recall, and f_1-score have been reported for the extraction task only, and the normalization-accuracy was the only additional measure. If the same measures were used for systems C and D in our example, it would be difficult to recognize that both systems perform equally well on the full task of temporal tagging. In contrast, in the TempEval-3 competition [UzZaman et al., 2013], the overall ranking of temporal taggers has been performed based on the f_1-score for the extraction and normalization.

STRICT AND RELAXED MATCHING

So far, we have assumed that temporal expressions can either be correctly extracted or not. However, since temporal expressions often consist of more than a single token, there might also be overlapping matches. Thus, for the extraction of temporal expressions, one can distinguish between strict and relaxed matching. In the former case, the extent of the extracted expression has to be identical to the extent of the temporal expression in the gold standard (e.g., the gold annotation *"Monday morning"* is the same as the system annotation *"Monday morning"*). For relaxed matching an overlap between the extracted expression and the one in the gold standard is sufficient (e.g., gold annotation *"Monday morning"* vs. system annotation *"Monday"*).

Note that the normalization might be correct independent of whether there is a strict or relaxed match. A complete evaluation of a temporal tagger should thus report evaluation results for the extraction and for the full task of temporal tagging based on both strict and relaxed matching. Since for many applications, a temporal tagger's output is particularly valuable if temporal expressions are normalized correctly independent of whether expressions are completely matched or not, relaxed matching with correct (value) normalization is often considered as the most important evaluation measure.

PROBLEMS WHEN EVALUATING TEMPORAL TAGGERS

There are two major issues that are typically not taken care of when temporal taggers are evaluated based on the above-described evaluation measures.

The first issue occurs when relaxed matching is used. Assuming that *"Monday morning"* is annotated as a single temporal expression in a gold standard corpus, a system might extract *"Monday"* and *"morning"* as two separate expressions. This is typically counted as one true positive and one false positive, for example, when using the official TempEval-3 evaluation script (see below). It is assumed that a single temporal expression can only result in one true positive. While this is intuitive as otherwise a system could extract more true positives than the number of temporal expressions in the corpus, this is also problematic. The system is penalized for extracting *"Mon-*

day" and *"morning"* instead of only one of them. A better solution would probably be to ignore one of the extracted expressions. Note that the difference between extracting the two tokens as two expressions and correctly extracting them as a single expression would still be reflected when calculating the evaluation measures with strict matching.

This issue becomes even more problematic if normalization is taken into account. Assuming that the value attribute of *"Monday morning"* is annotated as 2015-05-11TMO in the gold standard (TMO refers to "morning"). If the system assigns 2015-05-11 to *"Monday"* and 2015-05-11TMO to *"morning"*, this is counted as two false positives and one false negative, because the first occurring expression that is partially matching the gold annotation is typically used to determine if a system's normalization is correct. Intuitively, the temporal tagger performed quite well as the correct normalized value is determined, although the day information is determined twice. As the temporal tagger did not perform optimally, it should be penalized, but judging its quality with two false positives and one false negative seems to be counter-intuitive.

The second issue is due to the ambiguity of normalized values of duration and set expressions. Following temporal tagging annotation standards, the expressions *"one week"* and *"seven days"* should be normalized to P1W and P7D, respectively. As one week consists of seven days, assigning P7D or P1W to any of the two expressions could be considered as correct. However, existing evaluation scripts do not take into account that normalized values might carry the same meaning and normalizing *"seven days"* as P1W is judged as an incorrect normalization.

SUMMARY

In general, we agree with the TempEval-3 organizers that the *value f_1-score with relaxed matching* (i.e., correct *value* normalization combined with relaxed matching for the extraction) is the most informative measure to evaluate temporal taggers. Nevertheless, if temporal taggers are used in applications where (almost) only correctly normalized temporal expressions should be taken into account, the normalization-accuracy can be a good indicator together with the precision for the extraction task.

3.3 RESEARCH COMPETITIONS

As already pointed out, temporal tagging consists of two tasks, the extraction and the normalization of temporal expressions. To draw a comparison to general named entities, the extraction task is equivalent to what is broadly understood as *named entity recognition*, while the normalization task is equivalent to what is often referred to as the *resolution, normalization, grounding*, or *disambiguation* of named entities. While the first organized research competitions focused on the extraction task, later ones considered the full task of temporal tagging.

MESSAGE UNDERSTANDING CONFERENCES (MUC)

The first research competitions addressing the extraction of temporal expressions were the MUC (Message Understanding Conference) named entity recognition tasks in 1995 [Grishman and Sundheim, 1995] and 1997 [Chinchor, 1998, Chinchor and Robinson, 1998]. In addition to the three most common named entity types (*person, organization, location*), *numeric* and *temporal expressions* had to be detected by the participants' systems. The data sets that had been created for training and evaluation purposes contained English news articles, and for the annotation of temporal expressions, TIMEX tags were introduced, which later became the basis for the development of the TIDES TIMEX2 and TimeML TIMEX3 standards. To evaluate participating systems, the measures precision and recall were used.

In addition to the fact that only the extraction and not the normalization of temporal expressions were addressed in the MUC-6 and MUC-7 named entity recognition tasks, not all types of temporal expressions were considered. Only date and time expressions were included, and duration and set expressions were not. In addition, explicit and underspecified expressions were annotated, e.g., *"October 2010"* and *"December"* or *"Monday"*, respectively. Relative expressions were not part of MUC-6 but were added to the set of temporal expressions in MUC-7. There, however, only expressions relative to the timestamp of the document were considered, e.g., expressions such as *"today"* and *"last month"* [Chinchor and Robinson, 1998, Mazur, 2012].

AUTOMATIC CONTENT EVALUATION (ACE)

It took several more years until the first research competition was organized addressing not only the extraction of temporal expressions but also their normalization. In the ACE (Automatic Content Evaluation) time expression recognition and normalization (TERN) contest in 2004, as well as in the two follow-up contests in 2005 and 2007, temporal expressions had to be detected and normalized according to (first versions of) the TIDES TIMEX2 annotation standard. Starting with the TERN task in 2005, temporal tagging of not only news articles but also of weblog and discussion articles were addressed. Note that these types of documents are also typically written in such a style that the document creation date can be used as reference date for many underspecified and relative expressions.

While the ACE program was carried out in a multilingual way, the TERN task in 2004 only considered English texts—although some of the texts have been English translations of Arabic and Chinese documents. For the 2005 competition, temporal expressions in Arabic and Chinese documents were annotated without normalization information, and the evaluation was not carried out for Arabic [cf. Mazur, 2012]. Finally, in the 2007 TERN competition, there were participants for English, Chinese, and Spanish for the full task of temporal tagging.[5]

To evaluate the systems of the participants, the so-called *ACE value* was introduced to cover both extraction and normalization quality in a single score. All normalization attributes were

---

[5]Cf. http://www.itl.nist.gov/iad/mig/tests/ace/2007/doc/ace07_eval_official_results_20070402.html, [last accessed: Nov 9, 2015].

taken into account and weighted based on their importance. The measure was defined differently for ACE 2004, 2005, and 2007 [cf. Mazur, 2012]. Besides, this evaluation method is not used frequently outside of the ACE competitions for evaluating temporal taggers.

TEMPORAL EVALUATION SHARED TASKS (TEMPEVAL)

With the organization of the first TempEval competition in 2007 [Verhagen et al., 2007, 2009] as part of the SemEval series, temporal relation extraction became a major objective in the research community and the temporal markup language TimeML was used as annotation standard. However, in the first TempEval competition, temporal tagging was not offered as a subtask that needed to be addressed, but temporal tagging annotations were provided to the participants to address the more complex task of temporal relation extraction. Given documents annotated with temporal expressions and events according to the TimeML standard, the task of the participants was to develop systems to automatically determine temporal relations between events and the document creation time, between temporal expressions and events, and between two events in consecutive sentences.

In TempEval-2 [Verhagen et al., 2010] and TempEval-3 [UzZaman et al., 2013], temporal tagging as well as event extraction and their normalization were added as subtasks to provide research competitions for the full task of temporal information extraction. The goal of the temporal tagging subtask was to extract and normalize temporal expressions following TimeML's TIMEX3 definition. However, only the TIMEX3 attributes *type* and *value* were considered for evaluation purposes. For both competitions, the domain of interest was the news domain, that is, training and evaluation data were composed of news articles.

In the TempEval-2 competition, all tasks were offered in six languages (English, Spanish, French, Italian, Korean, Chinese) but only English and Spanish were addressed by the participants. As a result, the TempEval-3 competition was narrowed down to these two languages. With respect to the evaluation setup, there are also significant differences between TempEval-2 and TempEval-3, although, in both competitions, the extraction and normalization quality of temporal taggers was evaluated.

In TempEval-2, the temporal taggers' extraction performance was evaluated using precision, recall, and f_1-score at the token level. While this avoids the necessity of considering strict and relaxed matching separately, this results in the flaw that multiword temporal expressions are considered more important than single word expressions. This can end up in weird evaluation results, for example, that a system extracting four single word expressions (e.g., *"today"*, *"Monday"*, *"2002"*, *"March"*) achieves worse extraction results than a temporal tagger that misses all these expressions but correctly identifies *"the beginning of the year 2007"*, for which the first temporal tagger only extracts *2007* in addition to the single word expressions. The TempEval-2 evaluation is probably the only scenario in which temporal taggers are evaluated in this way. In TempEval-3, the measures precision, recall, and f_1-score at the expression level are reported for strict and relaxed matching.

To evaluate the temporal taggers' normalization performance, normalization-accuracy was reported in TempEval-2, while the f_1-score for relaxed matching was reported for the *type* and *value* attributes in TempEval-3. For TempEval-3, it was also established that the total ranking of the systems was realized according to the *value f_1-score*. As pointed out in Section 3.2, we also argue that this score represents a temporal tagger's overall performance in the best way and that this measure should be used to compare systems.

ITALIAN TEMPORAL TAGGING AT EVALITA

While the above-mentioned competitions all covered English either as the only language or as one of the languages of interest, in the context of EVALITA (Evaluation of NLP and Speech Tools for Italian), temporal tagging competitions were organized for Italian. In the 2007 competition, the extraction and normalization of temporal expressions were covered [Bartalesi Lenzi and Sprugnoli, 2007]. The training and the test data consisted of Italian newspaper articles, and TIMEX2 annotations were used as annotation standard. For evaluation purposes, a score similar to the *ACE value* score described above was used in addition to standard measures of precision, recall, and f_1-score for the extraction subtask.

In the 2014 competition [Attardi et al., 2015], the EVENTI (Evaluation of Events and Temporal Information) shared task was organized, in which the full task of temporal annotation was covered [Caselli et al., 2014]. The Italian version of TimeML, Ita-TimeML [Caselli, 2010], was used for annotating temporal expressions, and empty TIMEX3 tags were taken into account for the first time in any TimeML-based research competition. In addition to the standard training and test data containing contemporary news articles, a pilot study was performed using newspaper articles from 1914. For this pilot study, no training data was provided, and the goal was to determine how well temporal taggers perform on historic texts although they have been developed for a contemporary language [Caselli et al., 2014]. Following TempEval-3, the organizers chose to use precision, recall, and f_1-score for the extraction and type f_1-score as well as value f_1-score for the full task of temporal tagging, with the latter being the overall ranking score of the temporal tagging subtask.

I2B2 NLP CHALLENGE

All the competitions mentioned above focused on processing news- and news-style documents. In contrast, the Informatics for Integrating Biology and the Bedside Natural Language Processing for Clinical Records (i2b2) challenges address several NLP tasks in the biomedical domain. Shared tasks have been organized covering several NLP topics such as coreference resolution and relation extraction. The 2012 shared task addressed the topic of temporal relation extraction [Sun et al., 2013a], including event extraction, temporal tagging, and temporal relation extraction.

As data set, a corpus of discharge summaries was created. For the annotation, i2b2 annotation guidelines [Sun et al., 2012] were adapted from TimeML. The subtask of temporal tagging covered both, the extraction and the normalization of temporal expressions. In addition to extent annotations, the TIMEX3 attributes type, value, and modifier have been considered. The evaluation was done using precision, recall, and f_1-score for the extraction task, and the value f_1-score for the full task of temporal tagging. Normalization-accuracy was reported for all attributes for the sake of completeness.

With 18 participating teams, the challenge has been very successful. However, due to the varying topics addressed in each i2b2 shared task, this temporal annotation challenge unfortunately has been a one-time event so far.

CLINICAL TEMPEVAL

Like the 2012 i2b2 challenge, Clinical TempEval [Bethard et al., 2015] did not address the processing of news articles but the processing of documents of the biomedical domain. The documents of the Clinical TempEval competition are clinical notes and pathology reports. The goal was to provide a shared task for the full task of temporal annotation, that is, including event extraction, temporal relation extraction, and a subtask on temporal tagging. However, because the manual annotation of the training data was not finished on time [Bethard et al., 2015], the temporal tagging task only dealt with the extraction and classification of temporal expressions and the normalization was not considered.

As corpus, the THYME corpus [Styler et al., 2014a] was used, which was annotated according to the THYME Annotation Guidelines [Styler et al., 2014b], an extension of ISO-TimeML. A significant difference to ISO-TimeML and to the i2b2 shared task is that two new types of temporal expressions were added. Thus, in addition to date, time, duration, and set expressions, so-called *quantifiers* and *prepostexp* were used, covering expressions such as *"three incidents"* and *"postoperative"*, respectively. The participating systems were evaluated using precision, recall, and f_1-score with strict matching.

The Clinical TempEval competition was of limited interest with respect to the temporal tagging subtask due to the lack of normalization information for temporal expressions. For Clinical TempEval 2016, it was announced that the full task of temporal tagging would be covered,[6] but again only the extraction and not the normalization was considered.

QA TEMPEVAL

As a follow-up of TempEval-1, -2, and -3, QA TempEval also addressed the task of temporal annotation, but aimed at an extrinsic evaluation using (temporal) question answering instead of evaluating the single tasks of temporal annotation separately and independently [Llorens et al., 2015]. In addition to news articles, Wikipedia documents and informal blog posts were to be processed by participating systems.

The systems were evaluated based on the correctness of their answers to temporal questions (e.g., *Is <event-A> before <event-B>?*). To be able to provide answers to such temporal questions, the systems had to annotate temporal expressions, events, and temporal relations. However, due

---

[6]`http://alt.qcri.org/semeval2016/task12/` [last accessed: Nov 28, 2015].

to the extrinsic evaluation, temporal tagging performance was not determined in isolation and the varying challenges of temporal tagging of documents of different domains were not analyzed.

SUMMARY

In Table 3.3, we summarize the most important characteristics of the described research competitions including the number of participants addressing the temporal tagging tasks. As all the competitions rely on manually annotated data, several corpora have been developed for training and evaluation purposes. Note that except for i2b2 and Clinical TempEval, all competitions focused on evaluating temporal information extraction systems on news- or news-style documents. In the next section, we present these corpora and give an overview of further annotated corpora of the news domain. Temporally annotated corpora addressing documents with other characteristics than news-style documents will be surveyed in Chapter 4, where the challenges and solutions toward temporal tagging of documents from different domains are discussed.

3.4   ANNOTATED NEWS-STYLE CORPORA

Manually annotated corpora play a crucial role for the development and the evaluation of temporal taggers. In this section, we thus give an overview of English and non-English temporally annotated corpora containing news- or news-style documents. At the end of this section, the English and non-English corpora together with some characteristics are summarized in Table 3.4 and Table 3.5, respectively. Note that we include corpora containing neither TIMEX2 nor TIMEX3 annotations only if no other corpora exist for the respective language. Thus, we do not cover the corpora used in the context of the MUC competitions.

THE ACE (TERN) CORPORA

Although all training and evaluation sets of the ACE 2004, 2005, and 2007 time expression recognition and normalization contests were annotated using TIMEX2 tags, different versions of the annotation guidelines were used [Mazur, 2012]. Several data sets are released by the Linguistic Data Consortium, namely the 2004 training corpus for English, the 2004 evaluation corpus for English, the multilingual 2005 training corpus, and the multilingual 2007 training corpus.[7] The ACE 2005 and 2007 evaluation corpora are not distributed so far.

All publicly available ACE corpora are created in a similar format and there are official evaluation scripts, which can be used (after slight modifications) for evaluating temporal taggers. In the following, we briefly present the characteristics of the available corpora.

---

[7]ACE TERN 2004 English Training Data v 1.0, https://catalog.ldc.upenn.edu/LDC2005T07; ACE TERN 2004 English Evaluation Data v 1.0, https://catalog.ldc.upenn.edu/LDC2010T18; ACE 2005 Multilingual Training Corpus, https://catalog.ldc.upenn.edu/LDC2006T06, ACE 2007 Multilingual Training Corpus, https://catalog.ldc.upenn.edu/LDC2014T18 [last accessed: Nov 9, 2015].

Table 3.3: Overview of research competitions in which temporal tagging had to be addressed

Competition	Domain	Annotations	Language	Extr.	Norm.	Teams
MUC 1995	News	TIMEX	English	+	-	15[a]
MUC 1997	News	TIMEX	English	+	-	12[b]
ACE 2004	News	TIMEX2	English	+	+	5[c]
ACE 2005	News and Blogs and Discussion	TIMEX2	English	+	+	4[c]
			Chinese	+	-	2[c]
			Arabic	+	-	0[d]
ACE 2007	News and Blogs and Discussion	TIMEX2	English	+	+	4[c]
			Chinese	+	+	4[c]
			Spanish	+	+	1[c]
TempEval 2010	News	TIMEX3	English	+	+	8[e]
			Spanish	+	+	2[e]
			Italian	+	+	0[e]
			French	+	+	0[e]
			Chinese	+	+	0[e]
			Korean	+	+	0[e]
TempEval 2013	News	TIMEX3	English	+	+	9[f]
			Spanish	+	+	3[f]
EVALITA 2007	News	TIMEX2	Italian	+	+	4[g]
EVALITA 2014	News (Historic News)	TIMEX3	Italian	+	+	3[h]
i2b2 2012	Clinical	TIMEX3	English	+	+	18[i]
Clinical TE	Clinical	TIMEX3	English	+	-	3[j]
QA TempEval	News and Blogs and Wikipedia	TIMEX3	English	Impl.	Impl.	2[k]

Numbers of participating teams according to:
[a] Grishman and Sundheim [1995]; participants of the NER task,
[b] March and Perzanowski [1998]; participants of the NER task,
[c] Mazur [2012],
[d] Arabic was included in ACE 2005, but it was not evaluated [cf. Mazur, 2012],
[e] Verhagen et al. [2010], [f] UzZaman et al. [2013], [g] Bartalesi Lenzi and Sprugnoli [2007],
[h] Caselli et al. [2014], [i] Sun et al. [2013a], [j] Bethard et al. [2015],
[k] Llorens et al. [2015]; in addition, four off-the-shelf systems have been evaluated

The ACE TERN 2004 Training Corpus—English
The ACE TERN 2004 training corpus [Ferro et al., 2005a] contains 862 English documents from the news domain including 95 English translations of the Arabic Treebank and Chinese Treebank. The documents are annotated with TIMEX2 tags and contain 8,938 annotated temporal expressions.

The ACE TERN 2004 Evaluation Corpus—English
The ACE TERN 2004 evaluation corpus [Ferro et al., 2010] contains 192 news documents also annotated with TIMEX2 tags. It contains 1,828 annotated temporal expressions [Kolomiyets and Moens, 2009].

The ACE Multilingual 2005 Training Corpus—English, Arabic, Chinese
The ACE Multilingual 2005 training corpus [Walker et al., 2006] consists of English, Arabic, and Chinese documents. The 599 English documents are annotated with extent and normalization information and contain 5,469 TIMEX2 annotations. The documents are news articles but also texts from conversations, discussions, and weblogs are included.

For Arabic and Chinese, only extent information and no normalization information is provided in the original data sets. The Arabic and Chinese parts of the corpus are made up of newswire (40%), broadcast news (40%), and weblog (20%) texts. As for the English documents, the TIDES TIMEX2 standard is used for annotation. Although the Arabic part of the corpus consists of 433 documents, only 403 documents are adjudicated after a dual annotation phase and thus considered as "high-quality gold standard" by the developers [Walker et al., 2006]. These 403 documents contain 2,302 annotated temporal expressions. In the Chinese part of the corpus, there are 687 documents. 633 of them are adjudicated after a dual annotation phase and contain 4,986 TIMEX2 annotations.

Due to the lack of normalization information, Strötgen et al. [2014a] divided the Arabic corpus into a training set and two test sets consisting of 203, 150, and 50 documents, respectively. The small test set was re-annotated using TIMEX3 annotations, and normalization information was added to the expressions (the TIMEX3 type and value attributes). Note that due to many inconsistencies in the annotation of the original extents and several missing temporal expressions, the re-annotated, so-called (ACE 2005 Arabic) test-50* corpus contains 298 TIMEX3 annotations instead of the original 261 TIMEX2 expressions. Details about the three sub-corpora are given in Table 3.5. They are publicly accessible and thus can be used for evaluation purposes.[8]

The ACE Multilingual 2007 Training Corpus—Arabic, Spanish
The ACE Multilingual 2007 Training Corpus contains Arabic and Spanish documents. English documents are not included because no new training corpus was developed for English in the

---

[8]Using the original ACE 2005 Multilingual Training Data, the three sub-corpora can be reproduced including aligned normalization information. The required scripts are available after registration, see `https://github.com/HeidelTime/heideltime/` [last accessed: Nov 9, 2015].

context of the ACE 2007 contest. The 378 Arabic documents are news (60%) and weblog (40%) articles. In contrast, the 352 Spanish documents are all news articles. As in previous ACE corpora, temporal expressions are annotated with TIMEX2 tags. In addition to the extents, normalization information has also been annotated. However, since the data set was only released recently and because we do not have access to it, we cannot report the number of temporal expressions in the two data sets.

THE TIMEBANK CORPUS—ENGLISH

The TimeBank corpus was initially developed during the Time and Event Recognition for Question Answering Systems (TERQAS) workshop in 2002 as a reference corpus for TimeML [Pustejovsky et al., 2003b]. Thus, TIMEX3 tags are used for temporal expressions. In addition, events, temporal signals, and temporal relations are annotated. The TimeBank 1.2 version released by the Linguistic Data Consortium[9] consists of 183 English news documents with 1,414 TIMEX3 annotations.

For the TempEval-2 and TempEval-3 competitions, TimeBank was provided as training corpus [UzZaman et al., 2013, Verhagen et al., 2010]. In the context of TempEval-3, a cleaned and improved version of TimeBank was released,[10] currently containing 1,426 TIMEX3 annotations.

THE AQUAINT CORPUS—ENGLISH

Similar to the TimeBank corpus, the AQUAINT corpus[11] also contains news documents annotated according to the TimeML annotation standard. However, it "is not as mature as TimeBank 1.2 [...] [since the annotators] did not go through several rounds of annotation and annotation reviews" [Verhagen and Moszkowicz, 2008]. It contains 73 documents and 605 temporal expressions.

The AQUAINT corpus was used as an additional training corpus in the TempEval-3 competition, and a cleaned version is available together with the latest TimeBank corpus.[12] In this version, the 73 documents contain 652 TIMEX3 annotations.

THE TEMPEVAL CORPORA

In the context of TempEval-2 and TempEval-3, manually annotated corpora were created by the organizers. In addition to the corpora, official evaluation scripts are publicly available.[13]

---

[9]TimeBank 1.2 `https://catalog.ldc.upenn.edu/LDC2006T08` [last accessed: Nov 9, 2015].
[10]TimeBank (TempEval-3) `http://www.cs.york.ac.uk/semeval-2013/task1/` [last accessed: Nov 9, 2015].
[11]AQUAINT corpus `http://timeml.org/site/timebank/timebank.html` [last accessed: Nov 9, 2015].
[12]AQUAINT (TempEval-3) `http://www.cs.york.ac.uk/semeval-2013/task1/` [last accessed: Nov 9, 2015].
[13]Evaluation tools for TempEval-2 `http://www.timeml.org/site/timebank/tempeval/tempeval2-data.zip` and TempEval-3 `http://www.cs.york.ac.uk/semeval-2013/task1/` [last accessed: Nov 9, 2015].

The TempEval-2 Corpora—English, Spanish, Italian, French, Chinese, Korean
As described above, the TimeBank corpus was used as training data for English in the TempEval-2 competition—although in a different format than the original corpus. For the evaluation, new data sets were manually annotated. The evaluation corpus for the English temporal tagging task consists of 9 documents with 81 annotated temporal expressions. While this set was used to evaluate temporal taggers, an additional data set has been annotated to evaluate the temporal relation task because, for this task, TIMEX3 annotations were provided to the systems. Putting both sets together, the full English evaluation set contains 20 documents and 156 TIMEX3 annotations.

Besides English, the TempEval-2 data consists of Spanish, French, Italian, Chinese, and Korean training and test sets in which temporal expressions are marked with TIMEX3 annotations. While the development of this multilingual corpus was a big step toward multilingual research on temporal tagging (and temporal annotation in general), the organizers stated that one should not place too high expectations on the quality of the annotations in the non-English corpora:

> "It should be noted that for some languages the annotations are a bit experimental. For all languages but English, and to a lesser extent Italian, the TempEval-2 annotation was the first temporal annotation of this kind". [TempEval-2 release notes, Verhagen, 2011]

Fortunately, the annotation efforts have been pursued and resulted in high quality language resources for some of the languages as will be described below. In addition, Li et al. [2014] re-annotated the Chinese TempEval-2 data, because there were many temporal expressions without normalization information as well as several further annotation errors in the original data. The improved versions of the Chinese TempEval-2 data sets are also made available,[14] and are thus separately listed in Table 3.5.

The TempEval-3 Corpora—English, Spanish
In addition to the TimeBank and AQUAINT corpora, the TempEval-3 organizers [UzZaman et al., 2013] provided a large silver standard as training corpus. However, since annotations were created by automatically merging the output of three systems [Llorens et al., 2012b], the annotation quality is not sufficient in order to use the corpus as a benchmark for evaluating temporal taggers.

In contrast, the newly developed TempEval-3 platinum corpus[15] is of high quality [UzZaman et al., 2013]. However, as the test sets of TempEval-2, the TempEval-3 platinum corpus contains rather few temporal expressions compared to other publicly available corpora. In total, there are 158 TIMEX3 annotations in 20 documents.

---

[14]Improved Chinese TempEval-2 data `https://github.com/HeidelTime/heideltime/` [last accessed: Nov 9, 2015].
[15]TempEval-3 Platinum `http://www.cs.york.ac.uk/semeval-2013/task1/` [last accessed: Nov 9, 2015].

For Spanish, the Spanish TimeBank corpus (see below) has been split into a training and a test set. The two sets contain 175 and 35 documents with 1,094 and 198 TIMEX3 annotations, respectively.

THE SPANISH TIMEBANK CORPUS—SPANISH

In the context of the TempEval-3 competition, the Spanish TimeBank corpus [Saurí and Badia, 2012a] was developed. Note that initial annotations of these documents have already been used in the TempEval-2 competition, but they were improved in the context of TempEval-3. Besides the TempEval-3 releases, the Spanish TimeBank corpus is also distributed by the Linguistic Data Consortium.[16]

THE EVALITA I-CAB CORPUS—ITALIAN

The I-CAB corpus[17] is annotated following the TIDES TIMEX2 annotation guidelines with minor modifications to address Italian language specificities [Magnini et al., 2006]. The corpus was split into a training and a test set for the EVALITA 2007 competition [Bartalesi Lenzi and Sprugnoli, 2007]. They contain 335 and 190 documents with 2,901 and 1,652 annotated temporal expressions, respectively. The corpus contains news articles but—in contrast to most of the other temporally annotated corpora—the documents are from different genres of a newspaper (sports, economy, etc.) resulting in a broader variety of temporal expressions.

THE ITALIAN TIMEBANK—ITALIAN

While the developers of the Italian TimeBank corpus (Ita-TimeBank) described the annotation guidelines and specifications developed in the context of the corpus creation [Caselli et al., 2011], the full corpus itself has not been released as Ita-TimeBank corpus as of 2015.[18] In the context of the EVENTI 2014 competition, parts of the Ita-TimeBank have been used as training and test data as described next.

THE EVENTI CORPORA—ITALIAN

The EVENTI temporally annotated data consists of a main training set, a main test set, and a pilot test set, in which temporal expressions are annotated with TIMEX3 tags. The data sets consist of 274, 92, and 10 documents, respectively, and contain 2,735, 624, and 97 annotated temporal expressions. While the main training and test sets contain contemporary news articles, the pilot test set consists of historic news documents from the year 1914. All parts are publicly available.[19]

---

[16]The Spanish TimeBank corpus, https://catalog.ldc.upenn.edu/LDC2012T12 [last accessed: Nov 9, 2015]; the Spanish TempEval-3 data sets http://www.cs.york.ac.uk/semeval-2013/task1/ [last accessed: Nov 9, 2015].

[17]I-CAB corpus, available upon request http://ontotext.fbk.eu/i-cab/download-icab.html [last accessed: Nov 9, 2015].

[18]http://www.celct.it/projects/it-timeml.php [last accessed: Nov 9, 2015].

[19]EVENTI corpora https://sites.google.com/site/eventievalita2014/ [last accessed: Nov 9, 2015].

THE FRENCH TIMEBANK—FRENCH

The French TimeBank corpus [Bittar et al., 2011] contains 533 TIMEX3 annotations in 108 documents. All documents in the corpus are journalistic texts although they are sampled from different sub-genres such as local, national, and international news [Bittar et al., 2011]. The corpus is publicly available.[20]

THE MEANTIME CORPUS—ENGLISH, DUTCH, ITALIAN, SPANISH

The MEANTIME corpus [Minard et al., 2016] was developed in the context of the NewsReader project.[21] It contains 120 English Wikinews articles and their translations in Dutch, Italian, and Spanish. Temporal expressions are annotated with TIMEX3 tags, and the English, Dutch, Italian, and Spanish articles contain 525, 480, 507, and 486 annotations respectively. In addition to temporal expressions, further document- and corpus-level concepts are manually annotated, for example, entities and semantic roles as well as entity and event cross-document coreferences. The MEANTIME corpus was released in 2016.[22]

TRANSLATION-BASED TIMEBANK CORPORA—PORTUGUESE, ROMANIAN

For Portuguese [Costa and Branco, 2012] and Romanian [Forascu and Tufis, 2012], two corpora were developed in a similar manner. For Romanian, the English TimeML-annotated TimeBank corpus was translated and the annotations were aligned. Similarly, for Portuguese, the English TimeML annotated TempEval data sets were used (which is the TimeBank corpus except of one document). The Romanian TimeBank corpus contains—as the English TimeBank corpus—183 documents and 1,414 temporal expressions. As the English TempEval data set, the Portuguese corpus TimeBankPT is split into a training and a test set of 162 and 20 documents with 1,244 and 165 annotated temporal expressions, respectively. The corpora are publicly available.[23]

FURTHER NON-ENGLISH CORPORA—OLD SPANISH, CATALAN, INDONESIAN, ESTONIAN, HINDI

The increased interest in temporal annotation for languages other than English resulted in some further resources which can be used to develop and evaluate temporal taggers.

The ModeS TimeBank corpus [Guerrero Nieto and Saurí, 2012, Guerrero Nieto et al., 2011] consists of 102 documents from the 17th and 18th centuries written in Modern Span-

---

[20]French TimeBank `http://www.linguist.univ-paris-diderot.fr/~abittar/french-timebank/` [last accessed: Nov 9, 2015].

[21]`http://www.newsreader-project.eu/` [last accessed: May 15, 2016].

[22]The data sets of the different languages can be downloaded at `http://www.newsreader-project.eu/results/data/wikinews/` [last accessed: May 15, 2016]. The Italian part of the corpus will be available after the EVALITA 2016 competition as it is used as test set.

[23]The Romanian TimeBank corpus `http://www.meta-share.eu/` [last accessed: Nov 9, 2015]; the Portuguese TimeBank corpus `http://nlx-server.di.fc.ul.pt/~fcosta/TimeBankPT/` [last accessed: Nov 9, 2015].

ish. It is publicly available[24] and the documents contain 892 TIMEX3 annotations for temporal expressions.

The Catalan TimeBank corpus [Saurí and Badia, 2012b] contains 210 documents with 1,420 annotated temporal expressions. While most documents are news articles, the corpus also contains some texts of the genre fiction. As the ModeS TimeBank, the Catalan TimeBank is distributed by the Linguistic Data Consortium.[25]

The IndoTimex-Kompas corpus [Mirza, 2015] contains Indonesian news articles. It is split into a development set with 50 documents and a test set with 25 documents, but only the temporal expressions in the test set are manually annotated. The 25 articles contain 218 TIMEX3 annotations, and the corpus is publicly available.[26]

The EstTimeML corpus [Orasmaa, 2014] is a TimeML-annotated corpus containing Estonian news articles. It consists of 80 documents with 705 temporal expressions and is publicly available.[27]

The ILTIMEX2012 corpus [Ramrakhiyani and Majumder, 2015] is a corpus of Hindi news articles, in which temporal expressions are marked. The extents are annotated similarly to the TIMEX2 standard, and the expressions are classified as either Date-Time (D), Period (P) or Frequency (F). Unfortunately, no normalization information is added to the annotations. The 300 documents contain 1,919 annotated temporal expressions.[28]

MIGRATION FROM TIMEX2 TO TIMEX3

Due to the increasing popularity of TimeML and the large number of corpora annotated according to TIDES TIMEX2 annotation guidelines, there have been approaches to automatically migrate TIMEX2 annotations to TimeML. Saquete and Pustejovsky [2011] started the development of the T2T3 transducer to convert TIMEX2 annotations to TIMEX3. While they only performed a small evaluation using the TimeBank corpus and parts of the ACE TERN 2004 corpus, Derczynski et al. [2012] extended this work. They applied the new T2T3 transducer to several TIMEX2-annotated corpora and made the TIMEX3-versions of these corpora publicly available.[29] Unfortunately, the announced manually corrected versions of the automatically migrated corpora were not available as of the beginning of 2016. Thus, in the tables with the temporally annotated corpora, we only list the original TIMEX2-annotated corpora.

---

[24]The ModeS TimeBank corpus `https://catalog.ldc.upenn.edu/LDC2005T07` [last accessed: Nov 9, 2015].

[25]Catalan TimeBank `https://catalog.ldc.upenn.edu/LDC2012T10` [last accessed: Nov 9, 2015].

[26]IndoTimex-Kompas corpus `http://github.com/paramitamirza/IndoTimex/tree/master/dataset` [last accessed: May 15, 2016].

[27]EstTimeML corpus, `https://github.com/soras/EstTimeMLCorpus` [last accessed: May 15, 2016].

[28]ILTIMEX2012 corpus, available upon request `http://irlab.daiict.ac.in/ILTIMEXTagger.html` [last accessed: Nov 9, 2015].

[29]Converted corpora `http://bitbucket.org/leondz/t2t3/` [last accessed: Nov 9, 2015].

Table 3.4: English news corpora annotated with temporal expressions

Corpus Name	Topic	Standard	Doc.	Expressions
ACE TERN 2004 Training	News	TIMEX2	862	8,938
ACE TERN 2004 Evaluation	News	TIMEX2	192	1,828
ACE Multilingual 2005 Training	News, Weblog, Discussion, Conversation	TIMEX2	599	5,469
TimeBank v1.2	News	TIMEX3	183	1,414
TimeBank (TempEval-3 version)	News	TIMEX3	183	1,426
AQUAINT	News	TIMEX3	73	605
AQUAINT (TempEval-3 version)	News	TIMEX3	73	652
TempEval-2 (Temporal Tagging)	News	TIMEX3	9	81
TempEval-2 (Combined Test Sets)	News	TIMEX3	20	156
TempEval-3 Platinum Evaluation	News	TIMEX3	20	158
MEANTIME	News	TIMEX3	120	525

SUMMARY

There are several publicly available corpora annotated with temporal expressions—either according to the TIMEX2 or TIMEX3 standard. Although many of the corpora contain English texts, several corpora for further languages have been developed more recently. Note that all corpora presented above contain news- or news-style data. In Table 3.4 and Table 3.5, the corpora are listed together with their most important characteristics. In the next chapter, we address the topic of domain-sensitive temporal tagging and also survey temporally annotated corpora containing documents other than news articles.

3.5   SUMMARY OF THE CHAPTER

In recent years, there has been a significant increase in research on temporal tagging and temporal information extraction in general. It is important to realize that different evaluation measures and settings can be applied when determining the quality of temporal taggers, and that probably the most meaningful evaluation measure jointly considers the extraction and normalization performance.

In addition to the well-established annotation standards of TIDES TIMEX2 and TimeML with its TIMEX3 tags for temporal expressions, there also has been a wide range of research competitions that were playing a crucial role in moving the field forward. Many of the available temporally annotated corpora have been developed for these research competitions. In addition, several further temporally annotated data sets have been made publicly available. Al-

Table 3.5: Non-English temporally annotated corpora containing predominantly news articles (*Continues.*)

Language	Corpus Name	Standard	Norm.	Doc.	Expressions
Arabic	ACE 2005 Training	TIMEX2	-	403	2,302
Arabic	ACE 2005 Training-203	TIMEX2	-	203	1,137
Arabic	ACE 2005 Test-150	TIMEX2	-	150	904
Arabic	ACE 2005 Test-50	TIMEX2	-	50	261
Arabic	ACE 2005 Test-50*	TIMEX3	+	50	298
Arabic	ACE 2007 Training	TIMEX2	+	378	NA
Catalan	Catalan TimeBank	TIMEX3	+	210	1,420
Chinese	TempEval-2 Training	TIMEX3	+/-	44	746
Chinese	TempEval-2 Test (all)	TIMEX3	+/-	15	190
Chinese	TE-2 Training Impr.	TIMEX3	+	44	765
Chinese	TE-2 Test (all) Impr.	TIMEX3	+	15	193
Chinese	ACE 2005 Training	TIMEX2	-	633	4,986
Dutch	MEANTIME	TIMEX3	+	120	480
Estonian	EstTimeML	TIMEX3	+	80	705
French	French TimeBank	TIMEX3	+	108	533
French	TempEval-2 Training	TIMEX3	+	83	206
French	TempEval-2 Test (all)	TIMEX3	+	15	83
Hindi	ILTIMEX2012		-	300	1,919
Indonesian	IndoTimex-Kompas Test	TIMEX3	+	25	218
Italian	TempEval-2 Training	TIMEX3	+	51	523
Italian	TempEval-2 Test (all)	TIMEX3	+	13	126
Italian	I-CAB Training	TIMEX2	+	335	2,901
Italian	I-CAB Test	TIMEX2	+	190	1,652
Italian	EVENTI Train	TIMEX3	+	274	2,735
Italian	EVENTI Test	TIMEX3	+	92	624
Italian	EVENTI Pilot (historic)	TIMEX3	+	10	97
Italian	MEANTIME	TIMEX3	+	120	507
Korean	TempEval-2 Training	TIMEX3	+	18	287
Korean	TempEval-2 Test (all)	TIMEX3	+	4	95
Portuguese	TimeBankPT Training	TIMEX3	+	162	1,244
Portuguese	TimeBankPT Test	TIMEX3	+	20	165
Romanian	Romanian TimeBank	TIMEX3	+	183	1,414

Table 3.5: (*Continued.*) Non-English temporally annotated corpora containing predominantly news articles

Language	Corpus Name	Standard	Norm.	Doc.	Expressions
Spanish	ACE 2007 Training	TIMEX2	+	352	NA
Spanish	Spanish TimeBank	TIMEX3	+	210	1,322
Spanish	TempEval-2 Training	TIMEX3	+	173	1,092
Spanish	TempEval-2 Test (all)	TIMEX3	+	35	199
Spanish	TempEval-3 Training	TIMEX3	+	175	1,094
Spanish	TempEval-3 Test	TIMEX3	+	35	198
Spanish	MEANTIME	TIMEX3	+	120	486
Old Spanish	ModeS TimeBank	TIMEX3	+	102	892

though most of the early developed corpora focus on English, there are now temporally annotated corpora for a wide range of languages.

In the context of the description of some research competitions, we have already pointed out that there are domain-dependent challenges for temporal tagging. So far, however, we mostly surveyed temporal tagging of the most studied domain, namely news and news-style text documents. Thus, the overview of the corpora given in this chapter only covers temporally annotated data sets that contain such news or news-style documents. More recently, other domains or text genres have been studied in the context of temporal tagging, and there is a wide range of challenges that need to be considered when leaving the news domain. Thus, in the next chapter, we will discuss the challenges of temporal tagging of documents of several domains, including the most frequently addressed news domain.

CHAPTER 4

Domain-sensitive Temporal Tagging

Based on the theoretical foundations laid out in the previous chapters, we now explain the challenges of temporal tagging. As most of the research on temporal tagging so far dealt with temporal tagging of news and news-style documents, we will consider this domain first. However, after defining the concept of a domain from the temporal tagging perspective, we then extend this view by switching to other domains or text genres. In particular, we compare different text domains and their characteristics, which are crucial for building a suitable temporal tagging framework.

4.1 TEMPORAL TAGGING OF NEWS-STYLE DOCUMENTS

As described in the previous chapter, for quite a long time, news and news-style documents were the only subject of analysis in the context of temporal tagging. Such documents are typically written in standard language, and they are usually published at a specific date or time, the so-called *document creation time (DCT)*. Although all types of temporal expressions may occur in news and news-style documents, date expressions are particularly frequent. In addition, underspecified and relative references to points in time are often specified with respect to the publication date. While this is intuitive since news and news-style documents are typically read on the date of publication or closely later, we will ground our claims below when presenting the results of a cross-domain corpus analysis (Section 4.5).

In Figure 4.1, excerpts of the news article introduced in Chapter 1 are shown as an example of a typical news document. Obviously, the first task of a temporal tagger is to identify all temporal expressions. The second task is then to normalize these expressions. The normalization of explicit expressions is simple, but normalizing underspecified and relative expressions is difficult, because for all such expressions, a reference date or time has to be determined based on which the expressions can be normalized.

For many relative expressions in news-style documents, the DCT can be used as reference time—as in the example in Figure 4.1. However, further information is required to normalize underspecified expressions. To determine the relation to the reference time, in particular the tense information of verbs is helpful. Note that all underspecified expressions in the example refer to dates before the reference time, but this is just accidental, and references to the future also occur frequently in news documents. Determining the correct relation between an underspecified ex-

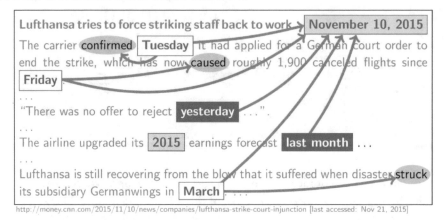

Figure 4.1: Example of a news document with arrows indicating required information to interpret the temporal expressions. Explicit, relative, and underspecified temporal expressions are shown in gray, blue, and white boxes. The document creation time and the verbs in gray ellipses help in the normalization process of the underspecified and relative expressions.

pression and its reference time is one of the main challenges in temporal tagging of news-style documents.

4.2   THE CONCEPT OF A DOMAIN

The objective of Chapter 4 is to describe the different challenges of temporal tagging of documents of different domains. Thus, it is crucial to first define the concept of a *domain* in the context of the temporal tagging task.

By introducing different domain types for temporal tagging, we aim at clustering documents that have the same characteristics relevant for temporal tagging. Thus, a *domain* in the context of temporal tagging is defined as follows (cf. Strötgen [2015]).

- In the context of temporal tagging, a *domain* is defined as a group of documents that have the same characteristics relevant for the task of temporal tagging.

There are numerous terms that can be used to name the concept of "a group of documents that have the same characteristics relevant for the task of temporal tagging", such as genres, registers, text types, domains, or styles [see, e.g., Lee, 2001]. However, the term "domain" fits quite well for the following reasons. (i) The alternative term "genre" is probably most frequently used to classify text documents, but it is usually assumed that the characteristics of documents that make them belong to the same genre are non-linguistic features [Biber, 1988, Lee, 2001]—a fact that is not valid in our case. Thus, we do not use "genre" to avoid any misinterpretation. (ii) The combination of two meanings of a *domain* according to the Merriam Webster dictionary[1] fits exactly our context: "a sphere of knowledge, influence, or activity" and "a region distinctively marked by some physical feature". On the one hand, a temporal tagger can be aware of different domains, that is, spheres of knowledge, and on the other hand, the text documents of every domain can be distinctively marked by some (linguistic) features as will be explained in detail in Section 4.4. In the following, we first survey temporally annotated non-news corpora.

4.3   ANNOTATED NON-NEWS-STYLE CORPORA

Analogous to the presentation of temporally annotated news corpora in the previous chapter, we now present temporally annotated corpora containing documents of other domains. This allows one to get a general idea of what types of documents are covered by existing temporally annotated corpora. A summary of the corpora with important characteristics is shown in Table 4.1 at the end of the section.

THE WIKIWARS CORPUS—ENGLISH

The WikiWars corpus [Mazur and Dale, 2010] consists of 22 documents with parts from Wikipedia articles about important wars in history. It has been the first non-news corpus annotated with temporal expressions, and it contains narrative texts and not news or news-style documents—an important difference to all previously developed corpora.

Note that while the number of documents is rather small, the texts are very long and rich in temporal expressions. In total, the 22 documents contain 2,681 temporal expressions annotated according to TIDES TIMEX2 annotation guidelines. WikiWars is publicly available[2] and formatted in the same style as the ACE corpora. Thus, the same evaluation scripts can be used to evaluate a temporal tagger's extraction and normalization quality.

FURTHER WIKIWARS CORPORA—GERMAN, VIETNAMESE, CROATIAN

Motivated by the WikiWars corpus, similar corpora have been developed for three languages, for which no temporally annotated data has been available before, WikiWarsDE for German [Strötgen and Gertz, 2011], WikiWarsVN for Vietnamese [Strötgen et al., 2014a], and WikiWarsHR for Croatian [Skukan et al., 2014]. Besides the fact that creating a corpus of Wikipedia documents serves for studying challenges that are different from news corpora, there are further advantages of building a corpus of Wikipedia documents. There are no licensing issues and documents in different languages that are similar to those of the original corpus in English can be easily determined using Wikipedia's interlanguage links.

As WikiWars, WikiWarsDE contains 22 documents annotated with TIMEX2 tags. Due to the shortness of the German Wikipedia article of one of the original articles, one document

---

[1]`http://www.merriam-webster.com/dictionary/domain` [last accessed: Dec 4, 2015].
[2]WikiWars corpus `http://www.timexportal.info/wikiwars/` [last accessed: Dec 4, 2015].

in the German corpus is made up of three articles about subtopics of the original article. With 2,240 temporal expressions, the German corpus contains slightly less annotations than the English corpus. WikiWarsDE is also publicly available.[3]

Due to the increasing popularity of TimeML compared to TIDES TIMEX2 annotations [Derczynski et al., 2012] at the time of the development of WikiWarsVN, the Vietnamese corpus is annotated using TimeML's TIMEX3 tags for temporal expressions. It contains only 15 documents, because for 7 of the English articles there was no Vietnamese Wikipedia document. In addition, the Vietnamese documents are much shorter and thus contain only 226 annotated temporal expressions. While the English and the German corpora have been annotated by two annotators, only one annotator performed this task for the Vietnamese corpus. Although these annotations were finally examined by this annotator and a TimeML expert without Vietnamese language skills, the corpus should be considered as "silver standard" according to the developers [Strötgen et al., 2014a]. Nevertheless, it is publicly available.[4]

The fourth corpus of this series is WikiWarsHR, the Croatian version of WikiWars developed by Skukan et al. [2014]. As in the Vietnamese corpus, temporal expressions are annotated with TIMEX3 tags. 21 of the 22 documents are built from the Croatian language-linked articles of the English documents, and one document is replaced as it did not exist in Croatian. Overall, there are 1,440 annotated temporal expressions in the publicly available corpus.[5] The previously mentioned TempEval-3 evaluation scripts can be used with WikiWarsVN and WikiWarsHR for evaluations.

THE TIDES PARALLEL TEMPORAL CORPUS—ENGLISH, SPANISH

Another corpus annotated according to the TIDES annotation guidelines is the TIDES Parallel Temporal Corpus. It contains transcriptions of 95 dialogs about arranging meetings in Spanish and their translations in English.[6] Although the corpus is rich in temporal information (more than 3,500 TIMEX2 annotations in both, the English and Spanish parts), it misses valuable information such as when the dialogs took place. Thus, underspecified and relative temporal expressions cannot be fully normalized due to missing context information, and the corpus is rarely used to evaluate temporal taggers. In addition, it is not available anymore.

THE TIMENEVAL CORPUS—ENGLISH

TimenEval is a small corpus of nine documents with 214 TIMEX3 annotations. It contains "a significant amount of non-newswire material" [Llorens et al., 2012a] in addition to some news documents. This mixture between news-style and non-news-style documents is problematic. Processing documents of different domains should be addressed by domain-dependent temporal tagging strategies as discussed later in this chapter. Either automatic domain detection on a docu-

---

[3]WikiWarsDE corpus `https://github.com/HeidelTime/heideltime` [last accessed: Dec 7, 2015].
[4]WikiWarsVN corpus `https://github.com/HeidelTime/heideltime` [last accessed: Dec 7, 2015].
[5]WikiWarsHR corpus `http://takelab.fer.hr/data/wikiwarshr/` [last accessed: Dec 7, 2015].
[6]The Spanish dialogs are part of the Enthusiast corpus [Suhm et al., 1994].

ment level needs to be addressed or a manual splitting of the corpus would be necessary to avoid problems. Then, however, corpora of different domains could be used for evaluation. In addition, due to further inconsistencies (e.g., DCT tags are not valid for full documents but only at the beginning of a document) and because of differences to other corpora with respect to normalization information (e.g., time expressions are normalized without date information although they refer to a time on a particular day), the TimenEval corpus should not be used directly for evaluating temporal taggers.

THE ANCIENTTIMES CORPORA—ENGLISH, GERMAN, FRENCH, ITALIAN, SPANISH, DUTCH, ARABIC, VIETNAMESE

In the context of a study on temporal tagging of texts about history, the AncientTimes corpus was developed [Strötgen et al., 2014b]. It is publicly available[7] and contains five documents for English, German, French, Italian, Spanish, Dutch, and Arabic, and four documents for Vietnamese. TIMEX3 tags are used to annotate temporal expressions, and in each language, at least one document covers each of the following time intervals: (i) before 100 BC, (ii) between 99 BC and 1 BC, (iii) between 1 AD and 99 AD, and (iv) between 100 AD and 999 AD. The documents, which are created from excerpts of Wikipedia articles, are about topics covering these four time periods, because these result in different challenges for temporal taggers that are rarely covered in other temporally annotated corpora.

TIME4SMS AND TIME4SCI CORPORA—ENGLISH

The Time4SMS and Time4SCI corpora were developed to analyze the challenges of temporal tagging of further types of text documents besides news articles (e.g., the TimeBank corpus) and narrative-style Wikipedia articles (e.g., the WikiWars corpus) [Strötgen and Gertz, 2012b].

Time4SMS contains 1,000 short messages of the NUS SMS corpus [Chen and Kan, 2013] and a total of 1,341 temporal expressions, that is, there are 341 temporal expressions within the text parts of the messages in addition to the 1,000 SMS timestamps. For annotating temporal expressions, TIMEX2 tags were used. The texts are very short and heavily colloquial and thus very challenging for natural language processing in general.

Time4SCI contains 50 abstracts of scientific publications about clinical trials. 317 temporal expressions are annotated with TIMEX2 tags—although significant extensions for the normalization of temporal expressions were required, because many relative temporal expressions cannot be anchored to real points in time. Details about respective challenges will be presented in Section 4.4.

For both corpora, the developers state that due to the very special domains, it is quite difficult to annotate temporal information in these documents without domain knowledge. Thus,

---

[7]AncientTimes corpus https://github.com/HeidelTime/heideltime [last accessed: Dec 7, 2015].

the corpora are viewed as preliminary versions toward a gold standard. Nevertheless, both corpora are available upon request.[8]

I2B2 CORPORA

The i2b2 corpus has already been used for a wide range of NLP tasks in the series of the Informatics for Integrating Biology and Bedside (i2b2) NLP Challenges for Clinical Narratives. For the 2012 challenge [Sun et al., 2013a], the corpus was enriched with temporal annotations including TIMEX3 tags for temporal expressions. In total, the corpus contains 310 discharge summaries with 3,224 temporal expressions.

The TIMEX3 annotations of date, time, and duration expressions are quite similar to the original TimeML definitions, but the normalization of set expressions (called frequencies instead of sets in i2b2) is different. The original TIMEX3 value and freq attributes are combined into one i2b2 TIMEX3 value attribute [Sun et al., 2013b]. The corpus including the temporal annotations is freely available but under a very strict license.[9]

THYME CORPUS AND CLINICAL TEMPEVAL DATA SETS—ENGLISH

The THYME (Temporal Histories of Your Medical Events) corpus consists of clinical notes and pathology reports of a large healthcare clinic. The full corpus contains 1,254 articles. Parts of the corpus have been manually annotated with temporal annotations covering temporal expressions, events, and temporal relations. Styler et al. [2014a] report details of the annotation process for a subset of 107 documents.

In the context of the Clinical TempEval 2015 competition [Bethard et al., 2015], further parts of the THYME corpus have been manually annotated. The data is organized into three sets, containing 293, 147, and 151 articles, respectively. The 293 documents of the training set contain 3,833 annotated temporal expressions, and the 147 documents of the development set (used as test data in the 2015 competition) contain 2,078 temporal expressions. The latest set was used as test data set in the 2016 Clinical TempEval competition and is now also available. The 151 documents contain 1,952 temporal expressions.

As briefly described in Section 3.3, TimeML was adapted to fit the clinical domain, for example, in addition to the four TIMEX3 classes (date, time, duration, and set expressions), two further classes (prepostexp, quantifier) have been added. Although annotation guidelines called "THYME-TimeML" have been developed (without information about how to normalize temporal expressions so far),[10] a detailed study of the annotations of the temporal expressions in the corpus showed that adapting the annotation of temporal semantics to clinical notes is rather challenging and that there is a wide range of inconsistencies in the annotations of temporal expressions [Tissot et al., 2015].

---

[8]Time4SCI and Time4SMS, https://github.com/HeidelTime/heideltime [last accessed: Dec 7, 2015].
[9]i2b2 corpus https://www.i2b2.org/NLP/DataSets/ [last accessed: Dec 7, 2015].
[10]THYME-TimeML http://clear.colorado.edu/compsem/documents/ [last accessed: Dec 7, 2015].

Table 4.1: Non-news corpora containing manual annotations of temporal expressions

Language	Corpus Name	Annotation Standard	Domain	Doc.	Temporal Expressions
English	WikiWars	TIMEX2	Wikipedia	22	2,681
German	WikiWarsDE	TIMEX2	Wikipedia	22	2,240
Vietnamese	WikiWarsVN	TIMEX3	Wikipedia	15	226
Croation	WikiWarsHR	TIMEX3	Wikipedia	22	1,440
English	TIDES Parallel	TIMEX2	Dialogs	95	3,541+
Spanish	TIDES Parallel	TIMEX2	Dialogs	95	3,764+
English	TimenEval	TIMEX3	News and Others	9	214
English	AncientTimes	TIMEX3	Wikipedia	5	311
German	AncientTimes	TIMEX3	Wikipedia	5	196
French	AncientTimes	TIMEX3	Wikipedia	5	290
Italian	AncientTimes	TIMEX3	Wikipedia	5	234
Spanish	AncientTimes	TIMEX3	Wikipedia	5	217
Dutch	AncientTimes	TIMEX3	Wikipedia	5	130
Arabic	AncientTimes	TIMEX3	Wikipedia	5	105
Vietnamese	AncientTimes	TIMEX3	Wikipedia	4	120
English	Time4SMS	TIMEX2	Short Messages	1,000	1,341
English	Time4SCI	TIMEX2*	Clinical Trials	50	317
English	i2b2 Corpus	TIMEX3*	Clinical Reports	310	3,224
English	THYME '15 Train	TIMEX3*	Clinical Reports	293	3,833#
English	THYME '15 Test	TIMEX3*	Clinical Reports	147	2,078#
English	THYME '16 Test	TIMEX3*	Clinical Reports	151	1,952#

* annotations of these corpora are significantly different from ISO-TimeML/TIDES TIMEX2.
+ according to Mazur [2012], after fixing several issues.
# The Clinical TempEval data sets of the THYME corpus do not contain normalization information for temporal expressions so far.

Similar to the challenges reported by Strötgen and Gertz [2012b] in the context of the Time4SCI corpus development, the THYME corpus developers also point out that "the process of normalizing those TIMEX3s is significantly more complex relative to the general domain, because many temporal expressions are anchored not to dates or times, but to other EVENTs (whose dates are often not mentioned or not known by the physician)" [Styler et al., 2014a]. For the 2015 Clinical TempEval competition, the manual normalization of temporal expressions therefore was not considered, but, according to the organizers, normalization information will be available in the future.

The THYME corpus is available for research purposes,[11] and the manual annotations for the Clinical TempEval data sets are distributed separately[12]—so far, however, without normalization information for temporal expressions.

SUMMARY

Temporal tagging research started with a focus on tagging of news articles and other documents in which the document creation time plays an important role (e.g., the weblog and discussion parts of the ACE 2005 corpora). In the meantime, there are also some publicly available corpora annotated with temporal expressions containing documents of other domains. For the annotation of temporal expressions, either the TIMEX2 or TIMEX3 standard has been used—although with significant adaptations for the corpora of the clinical (and scientific) texts. In Table 4.1, the corpora are listed together with their most important characteristics.

4.4 CHARACTERISTICS OF DIFFERENT DOMAINS

In the following, we describe the characteristics of documents of four domains that can be clearly distinguished in the context of temporal tagging. After the textual description, Table 4.2 on page 67 gives a summary of the main differences between the four domains. In addition to providing an overview of the characteristics, this also allows a direct comparison of the challenges of the domains. Details about strategies on how to address the challenges of the domains will be explained in Section 4.6.

4.4.1 NEWS-STYLE DOCUMENTS

The first domain we consider is the news domain. Figure 4.2 shows excerpts of two documents of the TimeBank corpus as two further examples of typical news-style documents in addition to the one shown in Figure 4.1 (page 48). As will be substantiated when presenting the outcomes of a comparative corpus analysis in Section 4.5, there are several features that are characteristic for documents of the news domain. In the following, we describe these features and explain them with the help of the sample documents.

Many Underspecified and Relative Expressions
A typical document of the news domain contains many date expressions, but explicit expressions (e.g., *"May 22, 1995"* in Figure 4.2) are rather rare. In contrast, many of the occurring date and

---

[11]The THYME corpus `http://thyme.healthnlp.org` [last accessed: Dec 7, 2015]. The data use agreement is quite strict due to the critical content of the corpus. For instance, the principal investigator of the applying research institute will be interviewed and must guarantee the data use agreement. This strict release process also led to a rather limited number of participants in the Clinical TempEval competition [Bethard et al., 2015].

[12]THYME annotations `https://github.com/stylerw/thymedata` [last accessed: Dec 7, 2015].

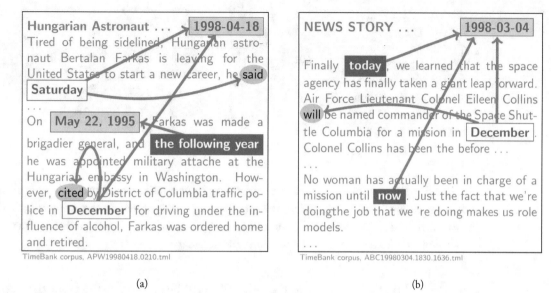

(a)   (b)

Figure 4.2: Excerpts of documents of the news domain. Explicit temporal expressions are marked with gray boxes, underspecified and relative expressions with white and blue boxes, respectively. Arrows and ellipses indicate information required for normalization.

time expressions are either relative (e.g., *"yesterday"*, *"last month"* in Figure 4.1; *"the following year"*, *"today"* in Figure 4.2) or underspecified (e.g., *"Tuesday"*, *"Friday"*, *"March"* in Figure 4.1; *"Saturday"*, *"December"* in Figure 4.2). Duration, time, and set expressions also occur but are much less frequent than date expressions.

The Document Creation Time is often the Reference Time

To normalize relative and underspecified temporal expressions, it is, in general, necessary to correctly detect their reference times. In documents of the news domain, the document creation time can often be used as reference time—as for all expressions with arrows to the DCT in the figures—except for those relative expressions with deictic behavior. For instance, *"the following year"* in Figure 4.2(a) is context-dependent and obviously refers to a previously mentioned expression. For such types of expressions, the reference time has to be detected inside the documents' text.

Tense Information for Normalizing Underspecified Expressions

As explained in Chapter 2, it is sufficient to detect the reference time to normalize relative expressions, but the relation to the reference time has to be determined, too, in order to normalize underspecified expressions. For the normalization of *"December"* in Figure 4.2(a), it is important

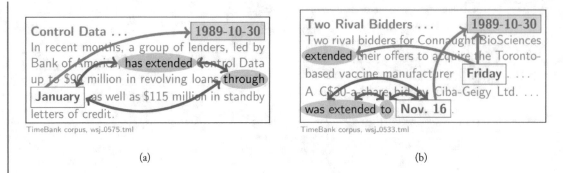

Figure 4.3: Tense information may be misleading to normalize underspecified expressions. Lexical knowledge about the verb, i.e., the meaning of *"extended"*, might help in the examples. However, only *"January"* in (a) and *"Nov 16"* in (b) refer to the future, and *"Friday"* in (b) refers to the past. Thus, a deeper syntactic (and semantic) understanding is necessary.

to understand that *"cited"* refers to the past and that "the citation" is the event that took place in December. Combining the information of the reference time and the relation "before"—due to the past tense—the expression *"December"* can be normalized to 1997-12. In contrast, the same expression in Figure 4.2(b) refers to the December after the document creation time, that is, the normalized value is 1998-12. The auxiliary verb *"will"* indicates that something will take place after the reference time, which is again the document creation time of the article.

Note that using tense information is often crucial to correctly normalize underspecified temporal expressions in documents of the news domain. Relying on other information such as the temporal distance between the underspecified expression and the reference time (e.g., "the December closest to the DCT") would result in one correct and one incorrect normalization in the given examples. This strategy would also fail to correctly normalize *"March"* in Figure 4.1.

Misleading Tense Information

Besides the issue that automatic approaches may sometimes fail to correctly perform tense identification, even correct tense information may sometimes be misleading. To avoid such issues, deeper lexical knowledge about the verbs and their prepositions can be helpful. For instance, in Figure 4.3(a), the underspecified expression *"January"* refers to the future although the tense of the sentence is present perfect (*"has extended"*). However, it is not "the extension" itself that took place in January, but something is extended through January.

In Figure 4.3(b), *"extended"* and *"was extended"* are both past tense (in active and passive usage), but *"Friday"* refers to the past and *"Nov 16"* refers to the future. In the first sentence, *"their offers"* were extended and "this extension" took place on Friday. In the second sentence, something was extended and "the extension" lasts until the upcoming November 16. Correct normalization in all these examples obviously requires a deeper understanding of the sentences including their syntactic structure and their semantics, and neither tense information nor lexical information alone about verbs is sufficient.

Note that sometimes even further background knowledge is required. For example, in *"The offer was extended to Monday"*, *"Monday"* could refer to a future or a past Monday with regard to the reference time, and the disambiguation is not possible by relying solely on information within the sentence.

Main Characteristics, Main Challenges

We can conclude that the main characteristic of documents of the news domain is that they are presented in a style that allows us to identify when they have been written or published. While many newspaper articles are written in such a way, it is important to understand that not only news articles but many other types of documents (e.g., letters and formal blog posts) are written similarly and thus belong to the same domain from a temporal tagging point of view. The main challenges for temporal taggers when processing documents of the news domain are to determine the relations between underspecified temporal expressions and their reference times, as well as to detect the reference time for those relative expressions for which the document creation time cannot be used.

4.4.2 NARRATIVE-STYLE DOCUMENTS

A first example of the narrative domain was already introduced in Chapter 1 showing excerpts of the Wikipedia article about "Heidelberg University" (Figure 1.2, page 5). An additional example of a typical document of the narrative domain is provided in Figure 4.4. It shows excerpts of the Wikipedia article "Soviet-Afghan War", which is part of the WikiWars corpus [Mazur and Dale, 2010]. Based on these examples, we explain the characteristics of the narrative domain in the following.

Many Explicit Expressions

While narrative-style documents such as Wikipedia articles also contain many date expressions, the differences to news-style documents are important. Explicit date expressions are much more frequent than in documents of the news domain (e.g., *"1979"*, *"summer of 1979"*, *"April 14, 1979"*, *"the morning of December 28, 1979"*, *"1978"* in Figure 4.4, and all date expressions except of one in Figure 1.2). Such expressions can be normalized without any context information once they are correctly extracted.

Reference Time Detection in the Text

However, relative expressions (*"the same year"* in Figure 1.2) and underspecified expressions (*"the spring"*, *"June 16"*, *"December 27"*, *"the morning"* in Figure 4.4) also occur frequently. In contrast to news-style documents, the document creation time is usually not suitable as reference time for such expressions. Thus, the reference time has to be detected in the text itself. For example,

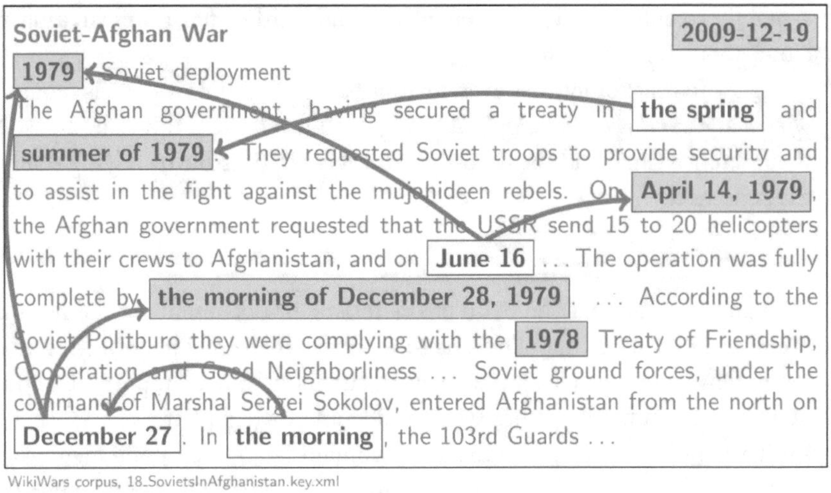

Figure 4.4: Excerpts of a document of the narrative domain. Explicit temporal expressions are marked with gray boxes, underspecified expressions with white boxes. Gray arrows indicate information required for normalization.

"1979" can be chosen as reference time for the expressions *"June 16"* and *"December 27"*—because it occurs as the heading of the paragraph. For both expressions, another previously mentioned expression (*"April 14, 1979"* and *"the morning of December 28, 1979"*, respectively) could also be used as reference time. Due to the presence of a coordination, *"summer of 1979"* can be used as reference time for *"the spring"*.

Reference Time Detection for Underspecified Expressions

It is important to understand that underspecified expressions can lack information at different granularities. For the three expressions *"the spring"*, *"June 16"*, and *"December 27"*, information about the year is underspecified. The expression *"the morning"* lacks information on day granularity. Thus, for this expression, *"1979"* is not suitable as reference time, because it is not specific enough. An expression of (at least) day granularity is required, and, in the example, *"December 27"* is the correct reference time. As mentioned above, sometimes, more than one expression is suitable as reference time. To correctly interpret *"June 16"* either *"1979"* or *"April 14, 1979"* and even *"summer of 1979"* can be used.

Often, the previous expression of a required granularity suits as a reference time. However, there are also expressions that are typically not well suited to be used as reference times, for example, *"1978"* should not be selected to normalize *"December 27"* although it is the previously occurring expression. A hint that it is not suitable is its attributive usage in *"the 1978 Treaty . . ."*, which may indicate that it is used as part of a name ("the 1978 Treaty of Friendship"). Thus, it might refer to a time outside of the chronological structure of the rest of the paragraph.

Determining the Relation between Underspecified Expressions and their Reference Time
Once the reference time is correctly identified, the relation between it and the underspecified expression needs to be determined. In contrast to documents of the news domain, tense information is typically not helpful when processing documents of the narrative domain. However, there are two promising assumptions to normalize underspecified temporal expressions in documents of the narrative domain. (i) The text part between the reference time and an underspecified expression is typically structured chronologically. Note that the assumption is not that a whole article is structured chronologically but only (usually) short passages between an underspecified expression and a previous expression determined as reference time. (ii) The expressions refer to dates that are very close to each other. Again, the assumption considers only the two involved expressions, which are typically close to each other.

Reference Time Detection for Relative Expressions
The strategy to determine reference times of relative expressions can be performed in an identical manner and works reasonably well when processing documents of the narrative and the news domain. For *"the same year"* in Figure 1.2 as well as for *"the following year"* in the news article shown in Figure 4.2(a), the previously occurring temporal expressions are suitable candidates. Note, however, that in both cases other temporal expressions—for example, expressions used as attributes—could have occurred in between the relative expressions and their reference times.

Error Propagation
A particularly crucial issue to recognize for the narrative domain is that an incorrectly chosen reference time for one expression may result in several follow-up errors. If *"1978"* in Figure 4.4 was selected as reference time of *"December 27"*, *"the morning"* would also be normalized incorrectly, because its reference time is chosen correctly, but normalized incorrectly. Note that error propagation is mostly a problem when processing documents of the narrative domain, because, in contrast to the news domain, the reference time has to be determined in the text for all underspecified and relative expressions.

Narrative Subdomains
A further difference between narrative-style documents and news-style documents is that the temporal scope of news-style documents is often quite limited to the present, the recent past, and near future. In contrast, narrative-style documents can also be descriptions about historical content, and thus expressions referring to dates of early centuries AD or even to any dates BC may occur frequently [Strötgen et al., 2014b]. These are rarely found in news-style documents.

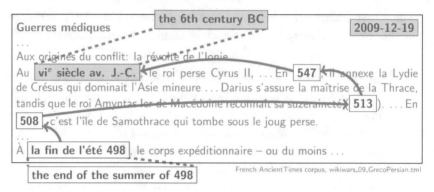

Figure 4.5: Excerpts of a French narrative document of the AncientTimes corpus (i.e., a document about history). Even temporal expressions with year information are not necessarily explicit due to missing information. All expressions in white boxes refer to BC-dates although no explicit phrase indicates that.

Thus, phrases to explicitly refer to "BC" and "AD" need to be known to correctly extract temporal expressions with such patterns.

However, it is also possible that temporal expressions are underspecified although they contain year information. In Figure 4.5, excerpts of a document of the AncientTimes corpus are shown, in which several temporal expressions refer to dates before Christ although this is not explicitly marked.[13] Thus, besides the need for additional vocabulary, a further challenge for temporal tagging of narrative documents such as those about historic content is that it has to be determined whether expressions refer to AD- or BC-dates if no explicit information is provided. This is a non-trivial task, and a simple taking over of time information is working fine in the example shown in Figure 4.5, but would fail in the example shown in Figure 4.6, a further example with excerpts of a document of the AncientTimes corpus. Here, *"30 BC"* should not pass its "BC-information" to following expressions.

In addition to the difficulties of distinguishing between AD- and BC-dates, two digit year expressions such as *"68"*, *"June 68"*, *"December of 69"*, and *"July 69"* in Figure 4.6 are even more ambiguous. They could be normalized to other centuries. In a current news document, these expressions would probably all refer to dates of the 20th century.

Main Characteristics, Main Challenges

In summary, the main characteristic of documents of the narrative domain is that they are typically written in such a way that the document creation time or publication time is not required to interpret underspecified and relative temporal expressions. In addition, narrative-style documents

---

[13]While this phenomenon may occur in many languages including English, we show a French document of the AncientTimes corpus, because in the English part of the corpus this phenomenon was not present.

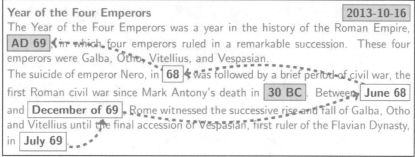

English AncientTimes corpus, ancient_YearOfTheFourEmperors.tml

Figure 4.6:   Excerpts of a narrative document of the English AncientTimes corpus. Determining if expressions without explicit AD and BC information refer to AD- or BC-dates is challenging. In this example, the explicit reference to a BC-date should not pass the BC information to the temporal expressions in the white boxes in the document.

often contain factual information and are typically quite long. Thus, they tend to have a rich temporal discourse structure, which makes the identification of the correct reference time for underspecified and relative temporal expressions more challenging [see also Mazur and Dale, 2010]. This issue as well as the fact that the reference time has to be determined for basically all relative and underspecified expressions (because the DCT is not suitable) are two of the main challenges when processing documents of the narrative domain.

4.4.3   COLLOQUIAL-STYLE DOCUMENTS

Documents of the third domain contain colloquial texts. Figure 4.7 shows excerpts of several short messages from the NUS SMS corpus [Chen and Kan, 2013], which are part of the colloquial-style temporally annotated Time4SMS corpus [Strötgen and Gertz, 2012b]. In addition to short messages, colloquial-style texts can typically be found in tweets [see, e.g., Gimpel et al., 2011, Ritter et al., 2011] or other textual social media content.

"Noisy" Language
A main difference from documents of the news and narrative domains is that colloquial-style documents often contain "noisy" language. There is a broad variety of spelling variations and word creations. Also for words with crucial temporal meaning this phenomenon occurs frequently.

The messages in Figure 4.7 are quite colloquial. Many temporal words such as *"night"* have multiple spelling variations in colloquial text, e.g., *"nite"* as in Figure 4.7(b), *"ni8"*, *"nit"*, and many more. The message in Figure 4.7(a) contains an additional example, *"tmr"*, which means tomorrow. Again, there are many more colloquial spellings and word creations for the meaning of tomorrow, such as *"tml"* or *"2moro"*.

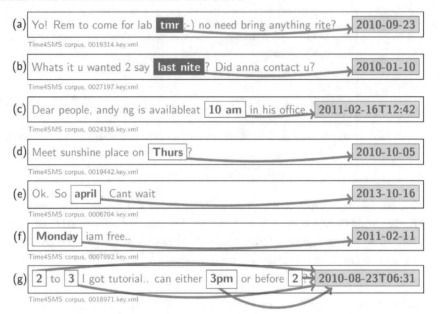

Figure 4.7: Excerpts of colloquial-style documents of the Time4SMS corpus containing short messages with relative and underspecified expressions in blue and white boxes, respectively. The gray boxes describe the DCT for each message.

Typing errors and missing spaces—-for example, *"availableat"* in Figure 4.7(c) and *"iam"* in Figure 4.7(f)—as well as dropped apostrophes as in *"cant"* in Figure 4.7(e) are also much more frequent than in non-colloquial documents. Finally, missing capitalization is a further feature of colloquial typing, for instance, *"april"* in Figure 4.7(e). Thus, when processing documents of the colloquial domain, these issues have to be taken into account and somehow addressed. In particular, the broad variety of spellings has to be considered, for example, by using synonym lists for relevant terms, that is, terms that might be part of temporal expressions.

Publication Time as Reference Time for Relative and Underspecified Expressions

The style of language is not the only difference between colloquial-style documents and documents from other domains. Date expressions are less frequent while time expressions are used excessively, especially in short messages (*"last nite"*, *"10 am"*, *"2"*, *"3"*, *"3pm"* in the examples). In addition, explicit date and time expressions rarely occur but underspecified expressions, for which the reference time has to be detected, are much more common. Fortunately, the time when a message was sent or posted (i.e., the document creation time) is usually the reference time for underspecified and relative expressions in short messages and tweets. For instance, the reference times of all expressions in Figure 4.7 are the respective sending times.

Missing Context Information

Unfortunately, sometimes one might also be faced with missing context information. For instance, *"10 am"* in Figure 4.7(c) could refer to the next 10 am with respect to the sending time—which seems to be reasonable—but if a previous message referred to another day, using the sending time as reference time would be the wrong guess to normalize *"10 am"*. The same holds for all four expressions in Figure 4.7(g) which are difficult to extract, too, because three of the four expressions are just one digit numbers. Once the expressions are extracted, one might guess that the day of the sending time is the day that the four time expressions refer to if there is no further context information available. But if another date was mentioned in the conversation, this guess might again be incorrect.

While a possible solution to address missing context information might be to process threads of messages together, access to the full thread might not always be available. Furthermore, different communication channels might have been used, for example, a meeting might have been scheduled via email and than postponed via a short message. In this case, even processing threads would not help.

Missing Tense Information to Normalize Underspecified Expressions

The normalization of underspecified expressions does not only require a reference time but also the detection of the relation between the reference time and the expression that is to be normalized. As in documents of the news domain, a good indicator to determine this relation is tense information. However, tense information is often either missing or very hard to detect in colloquial texts. The message in Figure 4.7(e) contains three sentences, and there is no verb in the same sentence as the temporal expression *"april"*. In Figure 4.7(f), "am" is hidden in *"iam"* and thus difficult to detect. Assuming that tense information was required to normalize an underspecified expression instead of the relative expression in Figure 4.7(a)—e.g., *"Rem to come for lab on Monday"*—it would be difficult to detect that *"Rem"* stands for "Remember" and is used as imperative. This would make a reference to the future much more likely than a reference to the past.

Further strategies to normalize underspecified expressions are obviously required in addition to only relying on tense information. As our corpus analysis (Section 4.5) suggests, and as all examples with underspecified expressions in Figure 4.7 indicate, colloquial texts such as short messages are often about the future. If tense information is missing when processing documents of the colloquial domain, the standard normalization of underspecified expressions should probably be to assign the closest possible future date or time.

Main Characteristics, Main Challenges

In summary, documents of the colloquial domain are written in such a way that the document creation time is crucial to fully understand the content. While this is similar to documents of the news domain, colloquial texts contain many informal spelling variations of terms including those that have some temporal meaning. Furthermore, tense information is difficult to access or not

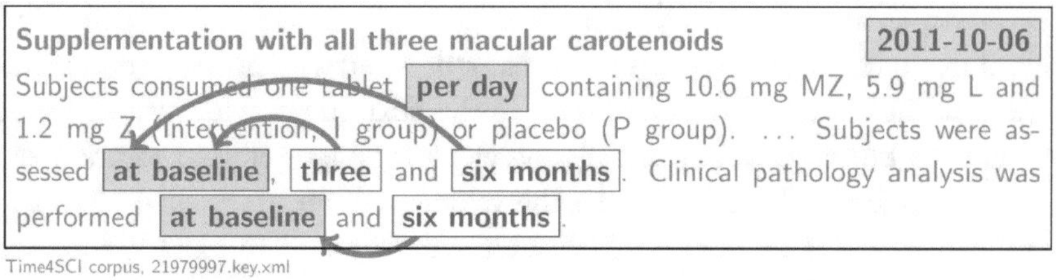

Time4SCI corpus, 21979997.key.xml

Figure 4.8: Excerpts of an autonomic-style document of the Time4SCI corpus.

available to normalize underspecified expressions, and thus an alternative normalization strategy is required. Due to the future-oriented style of colloquial texts in contrast to news-style texts, the strategy could be to use future dates and times as default normalization.

4.4.4 AUTONOMIC-STYLE DOCUMENTS

The fourth domain is named autonomic domain. In contrast to the other three domains, its naming needs some explanation. The main characteristic of documents of the autonomic domain is that they contain many temporal expressions that cannot be normalized to real points in time, but only according to some local or autonomic time frame. Thus, we consider all documents containing such a local time frame as being part of the autonomic domain. Examples of autonomic-style documents are specific types of scientific texts and literary works.

In the first work studying the temporal expressions in documents exhibiting characteristics of the autonomic domain, scientific documents about clinical trials were used, and the domain was thus called "scientific domain" [Strötgen and Gertz, 2012b]. However, while many scientific documents belong to this domain, documents of other genres may also be part of it. In the following, we present characteristics of such documents with some examples and point out the challenges for temporal tagging of documents of this domain. As the characteristics of the other domains, the ones of the autonomic domain are also summarized in Table 4.2, and strategies to address the challenges are explained in Section 4.6.

Date Expressions not Referring to Real Points in Time

In Figure 4.8, excerpts of a document of the Time4SCI corpus are shown.[14] In addition to a set expression (*"per day"*,) there are temporal expressions that refer to different points in time (*"baseline"*, *"three (months)"*, and *"six months"*). Note that *"three (months)"* and *"six months"* look like duration expressions, but they are clearly used to refer to points in time. These expressions, however, are used independently of the publication date of the article (2011-10-06), and the text itself also does not contain a real date for anchoring the expressions on a timeline. Thus, the

---

[14]The excerpts in Figure 4.8 are from the document of the Time4SCI corpus, which contains the abstract of the paper "Supplementation with all three macular carotenoids: response, stability, and safety" by Conelli et al. (2011), http://www.ncbi.nlm.nih.gov/pubmed/21979997/ [last accessed: Nov 2, 2015].

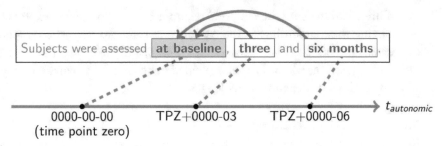

Figure 4.9: An autonomic timeline for the document shown in Figure 4.8 to normalize temporal expressions referring to points in time without referring to real dates according to a calendar.

expressions cannot—and are not intended to—be normalized to real dates according to a calendar but only with respect to the local or autonomic time frame of the document. The expression *"baseline"* could be defined as "time point zero" of the document, while *"three (months)"* and *"six months"* refer to time points that are three and six months after this time point zero, respectively. An example of an autonomic timeline is shown in Figure 4.9.

Time Point Zero Detection in Different Types of Texts
Examples of autonomic-style documents are scientific texts, e.g., documents describing clinical trials as the ones of the Time4SCI corpus. Literary works containing a local time frame also fall in the domain of autonomic-style documents. Note that there might be differences in suitable approaches to identify so-called "time point zeros". While expressions such as *"baseline"* are frequent in clinical trials, other clinical events such as operations may be time point zeros in other clinical notes [cf. Bethard et al., 2015].

Determining possible "time point zeros" in literary texts is more challenging since they might be highly content-dependent. In addition, longer articles may contain several local time frames, for example, an autonomic time frame per chapter or paragraph. For proper temporal tagging, this should be taken into account.

Covering Local Semantics of Relative Expressions
The key characteristic of autonomic-style documents is that they have a local time frame. There might be temporal expressions that can be normalized to real points in time while others can be normalized only with respect to a local time frame. Explicit expressions may also occur in documents of the autonomic domain. The goal of temporal tagging of documents of the autonomic domain should be to normalize those expressions that can be normalized to real points in time, as done in other domains. Expressions that cannot be normalized to real points in time should be normalized according to their local time frame.

Normalizing expressions such as *"six months (later)"*—if no real date anchor is available—as unknown point in time (XXXX-XX) as suggested by standard annotation guidelines results in a loss of information about the temporal relations between occurring expressions. We thus suggest normalizing them according to their local time frame to keep the temporal relations between expressions such as *"baseline"*, *"three months (later)"*, and *"six months (later)"* as shown in Figure 4.9. Detailed suggestions will be further explained in Section 4.6 when discussing strategies to address all kinds of domain-dependent challenges.

Many Duration and Set Expressions
Besides date and time expressions that can be normalized only with respect to a local time frame, there are further characteristics that can be detected in autonomic-style documents. For instance, duration and set expressions occur frequently in scientific documents such as in texts about clinical trials. However, due to the heterogeneity of texts being covered under the umbrella of the autonomic domain, we do not generalize the results of our comparative corpus analysis here, but discuss the characteristics of the documents of the Time4SCI corpus in Section 4.5 when presenting the outcome of a comparative corpus analysis.

Main Characteristics, Main Challenges
The key characteristics of documents of the autonomic domain is that they contain temporal expressions that do not refer to real dates but to points in time within a local time frame. Thus, they can be anchored only on an autonomic timeline. In addition, there might be anchors for relative expressions that are not standard temporal expressions, e.g., *"baseline"* in the context of clinical trials. Detecting such "time point zeros" is a tough challenge and genre-dependent.

Note that in contrast to the other three domains, the autonomic domain is less well defined and the explanations are rather imprecise. However, the goal of introducing an autonomic domain is that the meaning of (relative) temporal expressions should be captured as much as possible instead of just normalizing them in an unspecific way (e.g., *"three month later"* as XXXX-XX). Otherwise, this would result in the loss of valuable temporal information about the expressions.

4.4.5 FURTHER DOMAINS AND SUMMARY

When faced with the question *how many domains are there?* one might be tempted to answer *many* or at least *many more than four*. However, with respect to the characteristics that are crucial for the task of temporal tagging, the four domains described above already cover a very wide range of documents. In Table 4.2, we give an overview of the characteristics of documents of the four domains, the main challenges for temporal tagging of documents of each domain, and sample types of documents that fall into the domains.

Many Types of Documents are Covered by the Four Domains
Many types of documents are written in rather formal language and published on a particular date so that they can be temporally tagged as news-style documents. In addition to all types of news documents, (formal) emails and reports belong to this domain. Furthermore, many types of

Table 4.2: Characteristics, challenges, and examples of the four domains that can be distinguished in the area of temporal tagging

News Domain	
Characteristics	• Document creation time (DCT) plays a crucial role • Many date expressions • Many relative and underspecified expressions
Challenges	• Detection of relations between reference time and underspecified expressions • Detection of reference times for relative expressions where DCT is not the reference time
Examples	• News articles • Letters, formal emails, etc.
Narrative Domain	
Characteristics	• Independent of document creation time • Many explicit expressions • Often long texts with complex temporal discourse structure
Challenges	• Reference time detection for underspecified and relative expressions • Normalization of expressions referring to historic dates
Examples	• Wikipedia articles • Descriptive documents, biographies, documents about history, etc.
Colloquial Domain	
Characteristics	• Usage of "noisy" language • Rarely any explicit expressions • Document creation time plays a crucial role
Challenges	• Spelling variations and non-standard vocabulary • Detection of relations between reference time and underspecified expressions • Missing context information
Examples	• Short messages, tweets • User-generated social media content, informal comments, blogs, etc.
Autonomic Domain	
Characteristics	• Local time frame • Unresolvable relative and underspecified expressions
Challenges	• Validity of local time frames • Time point zero detection
Examples	• Clinical trials, clinical descriptions • Literary texts, etc.

documents belong to the narrative domain, because they are written in a rather formal language but mostly independent of the date of publication. Examples are documents about history and biographies, all kinds of Wikipedia documents, and descriptions.

Diverse types of user generated content such as short messages and tweets but also informal social media and blog posts can be processed as documents of the colloquial domain. Finally, the autonomic domain covers all texts that contain a local time frame and thus temporal expressions that are unresolvable in a conventional way.

Diverse Documents in the Autonomic Domain

Of course, a wide range of documents is in particular associated with the autonomic domain. On the one hand, scientific documents such as the ones discussed above about clinical trials belong to the autonomic domain. On the other hand, literary texts—which are typically quite different from scientific texts in many aspects—also belong to this domain.

Fuzzy Boundaries between Domains

The boundaries between domains are sometimes not straightforward or strict. Some literary texts clearly belong to the autonomic domain, because they contain many expressions such as *"on the next day"* or *"in the morning"* without specifying an explicit point in time at all, for example, the text of which an excerpt is shown in Figure 4.10(a). Other literary texts might better be considered as belonging to the narrative domain than to the autonomic domain, because many temporal expressions can be normalized to real points in time, for example, the one of which excerpts are shown in Figure 4.10(b).[15]

However, some literary works may contain both, relative and underspecified expressions that can be normalized using a real reference date occurring in the text, but also expressions that are unresolvable. Clearly, a major challenge when processing documents that cannot be unambiguously assigned to a specific domain is to choose the best fitting normalization strategy or to decide on the paragraph level or even on the expression level how expressions should be normalized.

4.5   COMPARATIVE CORPUS ANALYSIS—CHALLENGES FOR DOMAIN-SENSITIVE TEMPORAL TAGGING

To study the differences between domains with respect to the challenges for temporal tagging, we show the results of a comparative corpus analysis. This analysis also supports many of the above-described claims about the single domains. We use the following four corpora as representatives of the four domains: TimeBank (news), WikiWars (narrative), Time4SMS (colloquial),

---

[15]Temporal tagging of documents of the literary domain is so far hardly studied in the area of natural language processing. The first works on this topic have been performed in the emerging area of digital humanities, where Fischer and Strötgen [2015] studied references to dates of granularity day and month with explicit and underspecified date expressions in large literary corpora.

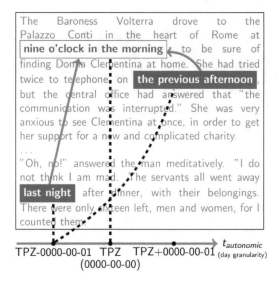

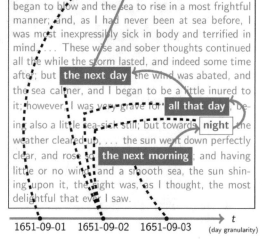

(a) Francis Marion Crawford, The Heart of Rome.

(b) Daniel Defoe, Robinson Crusoe.

Figure 4.10: Excerpts of literary texts, an autonomic-style (a) and a narrative-style one (b). Relative and underspecified expressions can be normalized to real points in time based on the explicit expression in (b); in (a), only a local time frame exists, and normalization is only possible on an autonomic timeline using a time point zero (TPZ).

and Time4SCI (autonomic). The corpora themselves have been introduced in Section 3.4 and contain news articles (TimeBank), parts of Wikipedia articles about well-known wars in history (WikiWars), short messages (Time4SMS), and abstracts of scientific publications about clinical trials (Time4SCI).

In addition to describing the characteristics of documents from different domains, we formulate the key challenges faced by a temporal tagger that is used to process documents of different domains.

CORPUS STATISTICS

Table 4.3 shows some statistics about the corpora. The documents of the Time4SMS corpus are very short with an average token number of 20. Although there may be longer colloquial texts, typical documents of this domain are short messages and tweets, which are both limited in their length. Thus, this characteristic can be observed for many colloquial documents.

The Time4SCI documents are similar to the news articles in the TimeBank corpus with respect to the average length (384 and 429 tokens, respectively). Note, however, that the Time4SCI

Table 4.3: Statistics of the four temporally annotated corpora that are used to analyze the differences between domains that are relevant for the task of temporal tagging

Corpus Domain	Content	Doc.	Tokens	TIMEXes	Average Tokens/ Doc.	Average TIMEXes/ Doc.
TimeBank (news)	News Documents	183	78,444	1,414	428.7	7.7
WikiWars (narrative)	Wikipedia Articles	22	119,468	2,681	5430.4	121.9
Time4SMS (colloquial)	Short Messages	1,000	20,176	1,341	20.2	1.3
Time4SCI (autonomic)	PubMed Abstracts	50	19,194	317	383.9	6.3

corpus contains only abstracts of scientific publications. Thus, documents of the autonomic domain may be much longer and also more complex to process.

Due to their shortness, documents in the Time4SMS corpus contain only a few temporal expressions (on average 1.3 expressions including the DCT). The numbers of temporal expressions in the clinical-trial documents and in the news documents are comparable—6.3 and 7.7 on average, respectively. In contrast, the 22 narrative WikiWars documents are very long with more than 5,400 tokens on average and contain many more temporal expressions than the documents in the other corpora, both on average and in total.

Although the Time4SMS and Time4SCI corpora are smaller than TimeBank and Wiki-Wars with respect to the number of tokens and to the total number of temporal expressions, their sizes are sufficient to discover significant differences between the corpora. Thus, they can be used to identify several challenges for temporal tagging of documents from different domains.

TYPES OF TEMPORAL EXPRESSIONS

To identify challenges for temporal tagging of documents from different domains, we analyze the temporal expressions occurring in the four corpora.

Document Creation Times

For each document in the corpora, there is a document creation time (DCT) provided as metadata, and the number of documents equals the number of DCTs. Thus, the fraction of DCTs among all temporal expressions in the corpora containing mostly long documents with many temporal expressions is very low (WikiWars), but very high for corpora with short documents

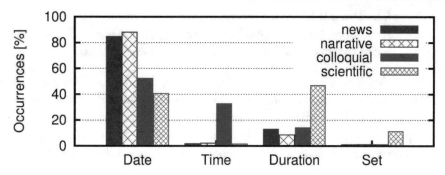

Figure 4.11: Distribution of date, time, duration, and set expressions in the corpora of the four different domains.

(Time4SMS). Since the DCT is provided as metadata of all documents in the four corpora, we concentrate on temporal expressions occurring in the documents' texts in our further analysis.

The detection of the document creation time from documents in which it is not directly provided as metadata, in particular from web documents, is a research field associated with temporal tagging [see, e.g., Tannier, 2014] that will be briefly discussed in Chapter 5.

Distribution of Types of Temporal Expressions

In Figure 4.11, the frequencies of the four different types of temporal expressions (dates, times, durations, and sets) are shown. In all four corpora, expressions of the type "date" are frequent. However, there are significant differences between the four domains. Temporal expressions of the type "date" cover between 40% of the temporal expressions in the Time4SCI corpus and almost 90% in the narrative corpus. In contrast, time and set expressions are only frequent in the colloquial and clinical trial corpora, respectively. Duration expressions are covered in all corpora although at a lower level than date expressions. Furthermore, duration expressions are much more frequent in the scientific corpus (which represents the autonomic domain) than in the other three corpora.

Temporal Tagger with Broad Coverage

Due to the differences in the distribution of types of temporal expressions in corpora of different domains, the following problem becomes obvious: developing a temporal tagger on one domain (e.g., on the typically addressed news domain) may result in a worse coverage when the system is used on other domains since not all types of expressions may be covered well. For example, it would be possible to extract more than 80% of the temporal expressions from the news and narrative corpora with a temporal tagger that only extracts date expressions. However, for the colloquial and scientific corpora only about 50% and 40% of the expressions would be extractable at all. Thus, a first challenge for temporal taggers designed for processing documents of different domains can be formulated as follows.

Challenge 1: Broad Coverage.
A temporal tagger designed for processing documents of different domains requires a broad coverage of all four types of temporal expressions.

Analyzing the distribution of date, time, duration, and set expressions already shows first significant differences between documents from different domains. However, these temporal expressions, and in particular date and time expressions, can be realized in different ways, and the types of realization again result in diverse challenges for temporal taggers. Thus, in the following, we study the distribution of their types of realization in the four corpora.

CHARACTERISTICS OF DATE AND TIME EXPRESSIONS

Temporal expressions of the types date and time can either be explicit, implicit, relative, or under-specified. In addition, in some types of documents, so-called unresolvable temporal expressions occur. The occurrence type directly results in different challenges for temporal tagging, especially for the normalization of temporal expressions.

To be able to analyze the characteristics of date and time expressions in documents of different domains, we manually assigned to each time and date expression in the four corpora its occurrence type [Strötgen and Gertz, 2012b]. For this, we followed the definitions of realization types of temporal expressions (cf. Section 2.3). Manually assigning the occurrence type to a temporal expression is a rather simple task, but it allows for an insightful comparison of the different domains. In Figure 4.12, the distribution of the occurrence types in the four corpora is shown.

Explicit and Implicit Expressions

Explicit temporal expressions, which are easy to normalize, are frequent in the WikiWars corpus ($> 50\%$) while they rarely occur in the colloquial corpus ($< 0.5\%$). In the news and the autonomic corpus, about 10% and 20% of the date and time expressions are explicit, respectively.

Implicit expressions are rare in all the four corpora. However, to be able to extract and normalize the occurring implicit expressions, the temporal tagger needs additional knowledge resources. For example, to extract and normalize holidays and expressions such as *"D-Day"*, the tagger needs to know these expressions in the same way as usual temporal words such as names of months. Thus, the second challenge for a temporal tagger can be described as follows.

Challenge 2: Resources for Implicit Expressions.
In some types of documents, implicit expressions occur frequently. Thus, there is the need to easily add resources to extract and normalize them.

Relative and Underspecified Expressions

To normalize relative and underspecified temporal expressions, for example, *"next Monday"* or *"November"* in *"In November"*, the temporal tagger has to identify the reference time of the corresponding expressions. In news-style and colloquial-style documents, the identification of the

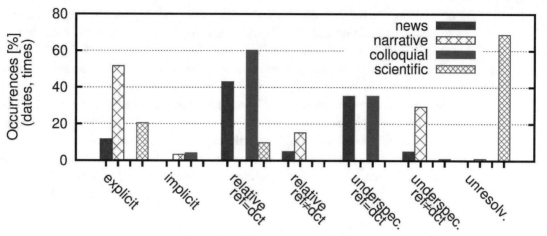

Figure 4.12: Distribution of the occurrence types of date and time expressions in the four corpora.

reference time is relatively simple since it is often the document creation time (DCT) or sending time, respectively. In narrative-style documents, almost always the reference time has to be determined from the documents' texts. The third challenge of a temporal tagger can thus be formulated in the following way.

Challenge 3: Reference Time Identification.

To be able to normalize relative and underspecified temporal expressions, a temporal tagger has to identify the correct reference time for these expressions.

Unresolvable Temporal Expressions due to Local Time Frames

In addition to explicit, implicit, relative, and underspecified temporal expressions, a further occurrence type of temporal expressions, namely unresolvable expressions, occurs frequently in autonomic corpora. Documents of this corpus often contain their own time frame, for example, the beginning of a clinical trial. This results in the fact that many of the temporal expressions cannot be normalized to some real point in time. Affected temporal expressions are in pa rticular relative ones, but also underspecified expressions. For example, a document of the Time4SCI corpus contains an expression referring to a point in time *"six months after the baseline"*. However, it is not intended that this expression is grounded to a real point in time, that is, to a specific date. The important information is that the expression refers to the point in time six month after a so-called time point zero (the baseline).

If temporal expressions cannot be normalized to some real point in time, the annotation guidelines of TimeML suggest that they are normalized in an underspecified way. For instance, if the expression refers to a date of the granularity day, the normalized value will be XXXX-XX-XX. Then, however, the temporal relation between *"baseline"* and *"six months later"* is lost. Thus, instead of normalizing such expressions to unspecific values, we suggest creating a local time frame for each document, and normalizing relative expressions with respect to the local time frame. While we already introduced the concept of local time frames above, we will describe how such a local time frame can be created and how relative expressions can then be normalized in the next section.

As shown in Figure 4.12, almost 70% of the date and time expressions in the scientific corpus are unresolvable expressions. Although such expressions rarely occur in the other analyzed corpora, dealing with this type of expressions is important when processing documents containing local time frames. Even though we only used scientific documents in our comparative corpus analysis, unresolvable temporal expressions also occur in literary documents and (fictional) narrative stories. Respective documents may contain several temporal expressions related to each other in a local time frame only. Thus, the next challenge can be formulated as follows.

> **Challenge 4: Local Normalization of Unresolvable Expressions.**
> In the autonomic domain, unresolvable time and date expressions occur frequently. These cannot be normalized to a global point in time and should be normalized with respect to a local time frame.

SUITABLE REFERENCE TIMES AND RELATIONS TO THEM

In Figure 4.12, we distinguish between relative and underspecified expressions for which the document creation time is the reference time (ref=dct), and those for which the document creation time cannot be used as reference time (ref≠dct). In the news and colloquial corpora, about 78% and 86% of the date and time expressions are either relative or underspecified, with the document creation time being the reference time. In contrast, only for 10% of the expressions in the news corpus the reference time has to be identified in the text. In the colloquial corpus, such expressions do not occur at all.

In the narrative-style corpus, almost 45% of the date and time expressions are relative or underspecified, and their reference time has to be detected in the documents' text, while less than 0.5% of the expressions have the document creation time as reference time. Furthermore, due to the large number of temporal expressions in the documents of the narrative corpus (cf. Table 4.3, page 70), the temporal discourse structure is more complex, and thus the reference time identification task is more challenging in this domain. In the scientific corpus, relative and underspecified expressions are unresolvable most of the cases. If they can be normalized, their reference time is usually the DCT.

In summary, it is often challenging to identify the reference time in narrative-style documents since it has to be determined from the text and is usually not the DCT. Thus, a temporal tagger should apply domain-dependent strategies to identify the reference time of relative and underspecified expressions in a suitable way.

Default Relations between Underspecified Expressions and their Reference Times

In contrast to normalizing relative expressions, for the normalization of underspecified expressions, it is not sufficient to identify the reference time, but the relation to the reference time is also needed. This is a challenging task when processing documents of all domains, and results in the fifth challenge for temporal taggers.

> **Challenge 5: Identification of the Relation to the Reference Time.**
> To normalize underspecified temporal expressions correctly, the relation to the reference time has to be identified in addition to the reference time.

As already mentioned in the previous section, if the DCT is the reference time of an underspecified expression (in particular when processing documents of the news and colloquial domains), tense information about the verbs in the sentence in which the expression occurs may be helpful. If the tense information cannot be identified, for example, because several short messages in the colloquial corpus do not contain any verb at all, the normalization will be even more challenging, and the relationship between the underspecified expression and its reference time has to be guessed.

News documents often describe events that already happened, but the analysis of the Time4SMS corpus suggests that colloquial texts such as short messages tend to refer to upcoming events. Thus, different default normalizations should be performed for different domains.

If the reference time is not the DCT, in particular in documents of the narrative domain, one may assume that there is a partially chronological order in the text, that is, an underspecified expression refers to a point in time after a previously mentioned reference time. Thus, domain-dependent strategies are needed to determine the relations between underspecified expressions and their reference times, in particular for processing news-style, narrative-style, and colloquial-style documents in which underspecified temporal expressions are quite frequent.

"NOISY" LANGUAGE AND ORTHOGRAPHIC VARIATIONS

In colloquial texts, further challenges arise that rarely occur in news, narrative, or scientific documents. These challenges include (i) a broad variety of spelling variations and word creations, (ii) typing errors, and (iii) missing spaces. Thus, if a temporal tagger aims at processing colloquial-style texts, it should be able to cope with orthographic variations and "noisy" language. This leads to the sixth challenge for temporal taggers that can be formulated as follows.

> **Challenge 6: Coping with "Noisy" Language.**
> In some domains, "noisy" language issues may occur frequently and have to be considered by a temporal tagger.

Examples of the first type of "noisy" language, that is, spelling variations and word creations, are synonyms for the word *"night"*, which we identified in the colloquial corpus Time4SMS: *"night"*, *"nite"*, *"nit"*, and *"ni8"*. While these terms occur in the corpus, more spelling variations can be found in colloquial texts. In addition, there are spelling variations for all kinds of words. To be able to perform temporal tagging on colloquial texts, at least the synonyms for temporally relevant terms have to be known by a temporal tagger. Otherwise, all temporal expressions containing informal spelling variations cannot be extracted correctly.

The other two issues mentioned above—typing errors (e.g., *"mornimg"*) and missing spaces (e.g., *"todaygot"*)—also occur frequently in the colloquial corpus. However, performing spelling correction on colloquial text documents is a non-trivial task due to the intentional usage of informal spelling variations. In the next section, we suggest some strategies to deal with these problems and present strategies to address these challenges. These issues usually occur only in colloquial documents and should be handled by the temporal tagger.

An additional challenge occurring in the documents of the Time4SMS corpus is that required context information may have been mentioned in previous messages but cannot be accessed for the normalization. For instance, in one of the examples in Section 4.4.3 (Figure 4.7, page 62, *"... andy ng is availableat 10am"*), we can only assume that *"10am"* refers to the next 10 am after the document creation time. While this seems to be likely, depending on the previous conversation, the expression could also refer to 10 am on another day. This issue can occur in every corpus containing parts of conversations. However, this challenge can only be addressed if the conversation (e.g., several short messages that build a conversation) is processed as a single document. Thus, this challenge is not a challenge that can be addressed by the temporal tagger itself, but may be addressed during the preprocessing of the corpus.

SUMMARY

Based on the observations of the comparative corpus analysis, we can summarize the challenges of temporal tagging as shown in Table 4.4. While some of the challenges are domain-independent, others arise only when processing specific domains. For instance, identifying the reference time of relative and underspecified temporal expressions is necessary to normalize such expressions independently of the domain. However, due to the different characteristics of the documents from different domains, it is necessary to tackle the challenges in a domain-dependent manner.

4.6 STRATEGIES FOR DOMAIN-SENSITIVE TEMPORAL TAGGING

In Table 4.4, the six challenges described in the previous section are summarized. In the following, we show how they can be addressed by a temporal tagger applying domain-dependent strategies.

GUARANTEEING BROAD COVERAGE OF A TEMPORAL TAGGER

Challenge 1, that is, a temporal tagger should cover temporal expressions of all types adequately, can be tackled if a temporal tagger is developed based on data of all domains. Either a machine

Table 4.4: Six challenges that have to be addressed by a domain-sensitive temporal tagger

Challenge	Description
1 Broad Coverage	All types of temporal expressions should be well covered by the tagger.
2 Implicit Expressions	Resources for implicit temporal expressions should be easily extensible.
3 Reference Time	For relative and underspecified temporal expressions, domain-dependent strategies to detect the reference time are required.
4 Local Time Frames	Some documents contain local time frames that result in problems when normalizing relative expressions with respect to current annotation guidelines. These expressions thus should be handled locally.
5 Relation to Reference Time	For underspecified temporal expressions, domain-dependent strategies to determine the relation to the reference time are required.
6 "Noisy" Language	Spelling variations, word creations, and typing errors may have to be addressed when processing specific documents, in particular colloquial texts.

learning-based temporal tagger should be trained using training data of all domains or the rules of a rule-based temporal tagger should be developed based on examples of all domains.

As the overviews of temporally annotated corpora in Section 3.4 and Section 4.3 show, many of the existing corpora contain news documents, and the other domains—so far—are less well covered. In particular, when developing machine learning-based temporal tagging approaches, one should make sure that sufficient training data covering all types of temporal expressions are used. Note that the broad coverage is rather independent of the normalization subtask. Of course, one should make sure that a temporal tagger knows how to normalize extracted temporal expressions, but the broad coverage of a temporal tagger first aims at a high extraction performance.

PROVIDING EXTENSIBILITY OF RESOURCES FOR IMPLICIT EXPRESSIONS

The second challenge listed in Table 4.4, that is, implicit temporal expressions can be integrated easily, can be solved if the architecture of a temporal tagger supports the simple integration of additional resources. While the vocabulary of standard temporal expressions is limited (e.g., it contains numbers and names of months and days), the vocabulary of implicit expressions is potentially unlimited. Thus, to extract and normalize these expressions, the temporal tagger should have access to resources in a modular way.

DETECTING REFERENCE TIMES OF RELATIVE AND UNDERSPECIFIED EXPRESSIONS

The first two challenges do not require domain-dependent strategies with respect to the implementation of a temporal tagger, but the third challenge listed in Table 4.4—the identification of the reference time of relative and underspecified expressions—should be addressed differently depending on the domain of the documents that are processed. In the previous section, we explained with some examples how reference times can be selected depending on the domain. In the following, we present the strategies in a concise manner.

A promising domain-dependent strategy to detect the correct reference time of relative temporal expressions is depicted in Figure 4.13(a). For documents of the narrative domain, the previously mentioned expression should be selected as the reference time of all relative expressions. In contrast, when processing documents of the news or colloquial domain, context-independent expressions (e.g., *"today"* and *"this month"*) should be normalized using the document creation time. Context-dependent expressions should be normalized as in narrative texts. For instance, *"the following day"* should be normalized using the previously mentioned expression. Thus, the strategy to select a reference time of context-dependent relative expressions is identical for documents of the news, colloquial, and narrative domains. In autonomic documents, the normalization is done based on the local time frame, and either a previously mentioned time point zero can be chosen as anchor point for the relative expressions, or a new time point zero is introduced for the relative expression.

Figure 4.13(b) shows a promising strategy to select the reference time of underspecified expressions (e.g., *"December"*). This strategy is less complex than the one for relative expressions, because there is no distinction between context-dependent and context-independent underspecified expressions. In documents of the news and colloquial domains, the document creation time is used as reference time for all underspecified expressions. Underspecified expressions in documents of the narrative domain should be normalized using the previously mentioned expression. Finally, in autonomic-style documents, the normalization is performed as for relative expressions, that is, according to the local time frame. Either a previous expression can be used as time point zero or the underspecified expression creates a new time point zero, which can be referred to by other expressions.

Note that whenever the strategy is to select the "previously mentioned expression" as reference time, one has to take care that the granularity fits. For example, if an underspecified time expression misses any date information (e.g., *"10 am"*), the reference time has to be of at least day granularity. More specifically, the "previously mentioned expression with fitting granularity" should be selected as reference time. In addition, we already mentioned that some temporal ex-

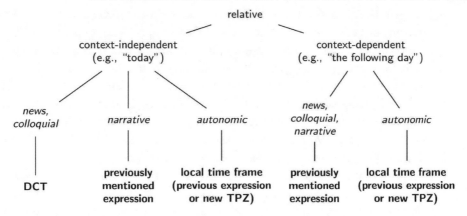

(a) Strategies to identify the reference time for relative expressions.

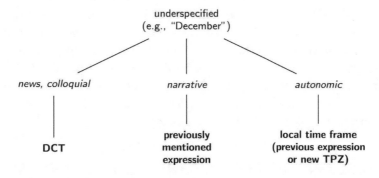

(b) Strategies to identify the reference time for underspecified expressions.

Figure 4.13: Domain-dependent strategies to detect the reference times for relative (a) and under-specified (b) expressions. Domains in italics, reference times in bold.

pressions might not be suitable for reference times, for instance, attributively used expressions such as in *"the 1979 Treaty"* (cf. Section 4.4.2, page 58). To determine if a temporal expression is a reliable candidate for a reference time or if it refers to background information is rather difficult and sometimes tricky. However, it might be useful to remove attributive temporal expressions from the set of candidates.

NORMALIZING UNRESOLVABLE TEMPORAL EXPRESSIONS WITH RESPECT TO THE LOCAL TIME FRAME

The fourth challenge listed in Table 4.4 is a complex challenge that mainly occurs in documents of the autonomic domain. In documents of the other domains, unresolvable expressions rarely occur—no occurrences in the TimeBank and Time4SMS corpora, 1% of the date and time expressions in WikiWars—so that one probably can justify to ignore them. As explained above, if unresolvable expressions are addressed, it is important that they are not normalized to unspecific points in time (e.g., XXXX-XX-XX), but with respect to a local time frame.

In order not to lose information about the relations between temporal expressions, we suggest normalizing such unresolvable expressions according to a local time frame, that is, a time point zero that has to be detected in the document. Note that this is only possible if the annotation standard for temporal expressions (e.g., TimeML's TIMEX3) is extended. We suggest using the local semantics of temporal expressions as defined by Mazur and Dale [2011], in which each temporal expression is first normalized locally. For instance, *"one day later"* is normalized to +0000-00-01. However, we suggest combining local semantics of expressions with local time frames of documents. Then, in cases of chains of relative expressions, the semantics can be accumulatively added. For instance, a document about a clinical trial may contain the following text *"… baseline… two days later … one day later"*. Then *"two days later"* could be normalized to TPZ+0000-00-02 and *"one day later"* to TPZ+0000-00-03 referring to two and three days after the time point zero (TPZ), which is also referred to by the notion *"baseline"*.

The documents in the Time4SCI corpus contain only one time point zero (if any), because the documents are rather short. Obviously, it should be possible to introduce multiple time point zeros in documents—in particular in long documents. For instance, think of a full scientific publication that is reporting on multiple clinical trials, then multiple anchor points are required to normalize temporal expressions accordingly.

DETECTING RELATIONS TO REFERENCE TIMES OF UNDERSPECIFIED EXPRESSIONS

For underspecified temporal expressions, in addition to the reference time, the relation to the reference time has to be detected (Challenge 5 in Table 4.4). A strategy how this can be achieved is shown in Figure 4.14.

If the reference time is the document creation time (DCT), that is, when processing documents of the news and colloquial domains, a promising approach is to use the tense information identified in the sentence. While the past tense indicates that the relation between the underspecified expression and the DCT is "before", the future tense and usually also the present tense indicate that the relation is "after". However, in some cases, there is no tense in the sentence, or the tense cannot be identified (e.g., in colloquial documents, cf. Section 4.4.3, page 63) and thus the relation has to be based on other information.

For this, we suggest a domain-dependent strategy. As described earlier in this chapter, news articles are more likely to refer to past events, while colloquial documents such as SMS and tweets tend to refer to future events, resulting in suggested relations "before" and "after", respectively.

In narrative-style documents, the reference time is not the DCT, and a promising assumption is that the expressions occur chronologically in the document. Note that this assumption is

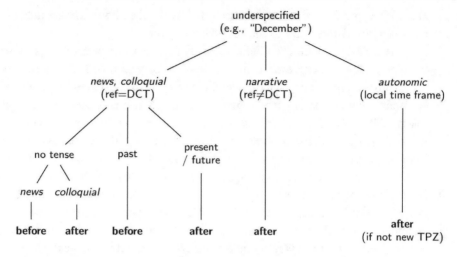

Figure 4.14: Domain-dependent strategies to identify the temporal relation between an underspecified expression and its reference time. Domains in italics, relations in bold.

not made in general for all temporal expressions in a document but only concerns the underspecified expression that is under consideration and the previously mentioned expression, which is determined as its reference time.

In summary, the normalization of relative and underspecified temporal expressions can be addressed by applying domain-dependent strategies for both, Challenge 3 and Challenge 5.

COPING WITH "NOISY" LANGUAGE

The sixth challenge listed in Table 4.4 is that a temporal tagger should be able to deal with "noisy" language. In contrast to the previous challenges, this issue mainly occurs in colloquial text documents and thus only has to be tackled when processing documents from the colloquial domain.

For spelling variations and word creations that refer to temporal expressions (e.g., *"tmr"* for *"tomorrow"*), we suggest adding the synonyms to the pattern resources of the temporal tagger. For this, online resources such as slang directories can be used. Then, informal spelling variations can be extracted and normalized by the temporal tagger as regular words.

A frequently occurring challenge that is more difficult to deal with are typing errors. As already mentioned above, standard methods to address this issue are not suitable since colloquial text documents usually contain intended informal spelling variations (e.g., *"tmr"*). Thus, a regular spelling correction tool should not be used to correct typing errors since intended informal spelling variations would be "corrected" as well. Therefore, we suggest adding all spelling variations to the dictionary of a spelling correction tool or tackling this issue by searching for inexact patterns. Depending on the length of an expression that is to be matched, one could specify a threshold and calculate edit distances, for example, the well-known Levenshtein distance [see, e.g., Manning et al., 2008, p. 58]. If the edit distance is below the threshold, inexact matches could be extracted and normalized according to the edited expressions.

A further variation of Challenge 6 that needs to be taken into account are missing spaces between a temporal expression and the previous or next token. While this issue could be seen as a variant of typing errors, we suggest addressing missing spaces by removing the generally used constraint that temporal expressions have to begin and end with the beginning and ending of a token, respectively. To avoid many false matches, one may want to validate that the whole token is not an existing word, for example, by using a dictionary. This would allow the extraction of *"today"* in the expression *"todaygot"* but avoid extracting *"May"* in the expression *"Maybe"*, for instance.

Since these strategies for coping with "noisy" language issues include modifications to the language resources of a temporal tagger, we suggest handling colloquial language as a separate language. For instance, when a temporal tagger is supposed to process English colloquial text documents, it could contain language resources for both English and English-colloquial. This also guarantees that the tagging quality on rather formal language documents will not suffer due to informal synonyms. Note, however, that we additionally suggest using different normalization strategies compared to the news domain so that a separate domain is required in addition to a separate language.

Similar to addressing "noisy" language due to phenomena occurring in colloquial texts, one may also want to extend a temporal tagger's vocabulary if documents about specific topics are to be processed, for example, narrative-style documents of the clinical domain [Bethard et al., 2015]. Such vocabulary extensions would, however, not influence the normalization strategies so that each topic with its own vocabulary does not have to be considered as a separate domain.

SUMMARY

In summary, it is crucial for a temporal tagger that is intended to process documents of different domains to be designed in such a way that domain-sensitive temporal tagging can be performed. In addition to domain-dependent normalization strategies for relative and underspecified expressions, several further challenges have to be addressed. Until some years ago, most approaches to temporal tagging dealt with documents of the news domain only, but works on temporal tagging of documents of different domains has been performed more recently and tackled some of the challenges [Mazur, 2012, Strötgen and Gertz, 2012b].

4.7   SUMMARY OF THE CHAPTER

In this chapter, we introduced the concept of a "domain" in the context of temporal tagging. Although a domain is defined differently in other contexts, we use the definition that a domain is "a group of documents having the same characteristics relevant for the task of temporal tagging". After surveying existing temporally annotated corpora containing non news-style documents, we showed that four domains can clearly be separated, namely, the news, the narrative, the colloquial, and the autonomic domain. By using a wide range of examples as well as a comparative corpus analysis with corpora of the four domains, we explained several challenges, and, finally, presented suggestions on how the challenges can be addressed.

After this theoretical description on how domain-sensitive temporal tagging can be performed, the next chapter gives an overview of state-of-the-art temporal taggers. In addition, the necessity of particular domain-sensitive temporal tagging strategies is shown through the evaluation of different taggers.

CHAPTER 5

Techniques and Tools

In this chapter, we switch from the more theoretical view on temporal tagging to the practical view. We describe approaches to temporal tagging and present an overview of existing temporal taggers. A special focus will be put on the aspect of domain-sensitivity, but we will also cover the aspect of multilinguality.

5.1 OVERVIEW OF APPROACHES TO TEMPORAL TAGGING

As there are two subtasks of temporal tagging, that is, the extraction and the normalization of temporal expressions, approaches to temporal tagging vary in the way the two tasks are addressed—either separately or in a combined manner.

The extraction task, that is, to correctly identify temporal expressions and their boundaries in a text document, can be regarded as a typical classification problem of deciding whether a token is part of a temporal expression or not. For this, approaches to extract temporal expressions range from rule-based to machine learning strategies.

The normalization of temporal expressions requires semantic knowledge and cannot be solved by simple classification methods. It is thus typically addressed using rules, which take into account contextual information (e.g., the document creation time, a previously mentioned expression, or tense information in the sentence) in addition to normalization information about the terms directly occurring in the expressions. Most approaches that rely on rules for the extraction make use of combined rules for the extraction and the normalization of temporal expressions. In contrast, machine learning approaches for the extraction task are typically accompanied by separate rules for the normalization. Obviously, the goal is that a temporal tagger can provide a normalization for all extracted temporal expressions—a behavior that can be guaranteed by combined rules.

More recently, semantic parsing approaches gained some attention. In these approaches, as will be described below, learning methods can be used to improve the set of extracted expressions and to rank possible normalization parses for the same expression.

RULES FOR THE EXTRACTION TASK

Rule-based approaches usually exploit some of the following features and techniques: pattern files, regular expressions, linguistic features such as part-of-speech information, positive and negative constraints, and a cascaded organization of rules. Some existing rule-based temporal taggers and their strategies will be detailed below.

The divergence of temporal expressions is very limited compared to the divergence in other named entity recognition and normalization tasks, for example, the number of persons and organizations as well as the variety of names referring to these entities are probably infinite. In addition to the limited vocabulary, a further motivation for using a rule-based approach is because of the two-fold tasks of a temporal tagger. It is intuitive to use the rules required for the normalization also for the extraction of temporal expressions. Thus, rule-based systems are frequently used to extract temporal expressions.

MACHINE-LEARNING FOR THE EXTRACTION TASK

Machine-learning approaches for the extraction of temporal expressions typically rely on a variety of features, which can be divided into four groups as suggested by Hacioglu et al. [2005] and Mazur [2012]: lexical features (e.g., token, part-of-speech, character-based features, frequency), syntactic features (e.g., base phrase chunks), semantic features (e.g., semantic role labels), and external features (i.e., tags of temporal expressions identified by other taggers). However, using tags of additional temporal taggers is rather atypical. If such external features are used, then they are only applied by machine learning approaches. In contrast, many of the other features exploited by machine learning approaches are often also used by rule-based systems. Many machine learning tools for temporal tagging also contain gazetteers of relevant terms, that is, handcrafted lists of temporal words.

Based on the features, a range of different machine learning techniques can be trained using some training data, that is, temporally annotated corpora. The task can then be modeled as IOB classification (also referred to as BIO classification) to decide for each token whether it is inside of a temporal expression (I), outside of a temporal expression (O), or at the beginning of a temporal expression (B). An alternative is to classify constituents of a parse tree, that is, to perform a binary constituent-based classification. Instead of individual tokens, entire phrases are either labeled as temporal expression or not.

Some of the machine learning methods, which have been frequently applied for the task of temporal tagging, are maximum entropy classifiers, support vector machines, and conditional random fields. In addition to rule-based systems, we present some existing temporal taggers that rely on machine learning methods for the extraction task in the next section.

RULE-BASED VS. MACHINE-LEARNING APPROACHES

A big advantage of handcrafted rules for the extraction task is that rules can be easily modified and new rules can be added whenever necessary. Machine learning approaches typically rely on trained models that are learned based on annotations in a training corpus. Thus, they are difficult to modify and tailored modifications are hardly possible. An alternative to modifications is to retrain the model, for example, if additional training data is available. However, a retraining of a machine learning model does not necessarily mean that specific expressions will be learned correctly although they occur in the (added) training data. On the one hand, the set of temporal expressions extracted by handcrafted rules is thus more predictable than the set of expressions identified by machine learning methods. On the other hand, machine learning systems may be able to generalize better.

Although a temporal tagger's rule base for a specific language is usually created based on some training data, annotation guidelines and language knowledge alone are often sufficient to develop temporal tagging capacities in the form of rules for a specific language. That is, a training corpus helps to develop a rule-based system or to extend it to a new language but it is not necessary. In contrast, machine learning techniques require training data for each language, but less time to develop the model itself, for instance, when additional languages shall be addressed. However, the development of manually annotated corpora is quite time-consuming and requires knowledge about the language.

In the TempEval competitions, in which temporal taggers were evaluated on news corpora, the extraction performance of rule-based systems and machine-learning approaches were quite similar. For instance, a statistical system performed the best at strict matching and a rule-engineered system the best at relaxed matching. Overall, the TempEval-3 organizers conclude "that rule-engineering and machine learning are equally good at timex recognition" [UzZaman et al., 2013].

RULES FOR THE NORMALIZATION TASK

The goal of normalizing temporal expressions is to capture their temporal meaning. Thus, values in some standard format—usually following specific annotation guidelines (cf. Section 3.1)—for several attributes are assigned to each temporal expression. This is a more challenging and complex task than the extraction, because no direct classification can be applied due to the non-finite number of possible values, and because of the need to perform calendar-based calculations. Thus, almost all temporal taggers address the normalization task in a rule-based way. In summary, existing temporal taggers use either a combination of machine learning and rule-based approaches or exclusively rule-based methods.

SEMANTIC PARSING OF TEMPORAL EXPRESSIONS

Intuitively, the handcrafted rules of rule-based approaches described above can be considered as formal grammars, and thus they can also be formalized using semantic grammar formalisms such as Combinatory Categorial Grammars. Models to extract temporal expressions based on parsing output and the ranking of competing parses to normalize temporal expressions can be learned separately. Note, however, that the formalization of the grammar, that is, the entries of a grammar's lexicon, is performed in a manual way before learning approaches are applied. The learning during the extraction phase is performed to prune the set of extractions and to resolve conflicts between overlapping expressions, while the learning during the normalization phase aims at ranking the possible meanings (normalized values) of ambiguous temporal expressions. More details will be given below when presenting a temporal tagger that realizes this strategy (Section 5.2.4).

DOCUMENT TYPES AND LANGUAGES

While there has been a lot of research on temporal tagging in the last years, almost always news or news-style documents were addressed. This, however, is problematic due to different characteristics of text documents from different domains, as was discussed in detail in the previous chapter. Similarly, most of the research on temporal tagging deals with English as the only language. While research competitions have aimed at motivating research on languages different from English by organizing tasks for several languages, there are still many temporal taggers addressing English as the only language. In Section 5.5, we will discuss the aspect of multilingual temporal tagging in more detail.

5.2   OVERVIEW OF EXISTING TEMPORAL TAGGERS

At the beginning of research on temporal tagging, some approaches to temporal tagging were suggested. With GUTime [Verhagen et al., 2005], only one temporal tagger was made publicly available and was frequently used by researchers of different research fields to exploit temporal tagging output. GUTime was built as an extension of TempEx [Mani and Wilson, 2000a] and was developed as reference tool for TimeML using TIMEX3 tags. It also became part of TARSQI [Verhagen and Pustejovsky, 2008, 2012], a toolkit that aims at the full task of temporal annotation according to the TimeML specifications with components for the extraction of events, temporal expressions, and temporal relations. GUTime is a rather simple rule-based system that can extract explicit expressions as well as relative and underspecified expressions. However, for normalizing the latter ones, the document creation time is typically used as reference time and no further context information is considered.

EARLY SYSTEMS FOR TEMPORAL TAGGING

Several further tools have been developed in particular in the context of temporal tagging competitions. While some of them addressed more than one language, all temporal taggers aimed at processing news-style documents. Systems relying on machine learning for the extraction use, for instance, support vector machines for token-level classification (English and Chinese, extraction only) [Hacioglu et al., 2005] or maximum entropy classification for constituents of parse trees (English) [Kolomiyets and Moens, 2009]. Some machine learning systems were combined with a normalization component or were later extended to cover the normalization of temporal expressions [e.g., Kolomiyets and Moens, 2010].

Examples of rule-based system covering the extraction and normalization are Chronos for English and Italian [Negri and Marseglia, 2004], TERSEO [Saquete et al., 2006], which was initially developed for Spanish and semi-automatically extended to further languages such as English and Italian, as well as DANTE [Mazur and Dale, 2009] for processing English documents.

TOWARD DOMAIN-SENSITIVE TEMPORAL TAGGING

DANTE was initially developed with a normalization strategy tailored toward the processing of news documents [Mazur and Dale, 2009]. The developers of DANTE then showed on the Wiki-Wars corpus of manually annotated Wikipedia documents that this strategy results in a significant drop of the normalization quality when switching the domain of the documents that are to be processed [Mazur and Dale, 2010]. For this, they later extended DANTE by implementing a second normalization strategy so that news- and narrative-style documents can be processed successfully with high extraction and normalization quality [Mazur, 2012]. When processing documents of the news domain, the document creation time is used as reference time for underspecified and relative temporal expressions while the previously occurring expression is used when processing narrative-style documents. The domain-sensitive temporal tagger DANTE is only available upon request[1] and runs only in combination with several other components within a GATE processing pipeline. Therefore, it is not frequently used by other researchers or as input for other applications.

FULL-FLEDGED, READY-TO-USE TEMPORAL TAGGERS

Nowadays, there are several temporal taggers publicly available and the above-mentioned tools including GUTime are hardly used anymore. Since our goal is to present the state-of-the-art of temporal tagging systems that can directly be applied, we present the following publicly available temporal taggers: TIPSem (Section 5.2.1), HeidelTime (Section 5.2.2), SUTime (Section 5.2.3), and UWTime (Section 5.2.4). In Section 5.2.5, we compare these tools with each other with a special focus on domain-sensitivity and multilinguality, and discuss their evaluation performance.

5.2.1 TIPSEM—EXPLOITING SEMANTIC INFORMATION

TIPSem was developed at the University of Alicante in the context of TempEval-2 for processing English and Spanish news-style documents [Llorens et al., 2010]. It uses Conditional Random Fields trained on annotated corpora, and it puts a special focus on semantic information—in particular by exploiting semantic role and semantic network information. While the same features have been used for developing the English and the Spanish models, both are trained relying on their own annotated training data. For this, the TempEval-2 training sets have been used. The classification of temporal expressions into one of the four TimeML classes (date, time, duration, and set) is addressed in the same way as the extraction except that the features are not used on the token level but on the expression level. Finally, the normalization is solved in a rule-based manner. TIPSem does not distinguish between documents of different domains and thus uses the document creation time as reference time to normalize underspecified and relative expressions.

---

[1]DANTE is available upon request, `http://timexportal.wikidot.com/dante` [last accessed: Jan 4, 2016].

TIPSem performs the full task of temporal annotation according to the TimeML specifications, that is, not only temporal tagging is addressed but also event extraction and temporal relation extraction. Furthermore, in addition to the full-featured system, a baseline system (TIPSemB) relying only on morpho-syntactic features was developed.

At the TempEval-2 challenge, TIPSem performed well and achieved the best results for several subtasks, including Spanish temporal tagging [Verhagen et al., 2010]. Comparing the results of TIPSem and TIPSemB, Llorens et al. [2010] showed that the semantic features help to build models that generalize better. While the precision values of both systems were quite similar, the recall of the full-featured system was significantly higher.

TIPSem is implemented in Java and publicly available for non-commercial educational and research purposes.[2] Note that the TIPSemB models are directly available but the TIPSem models only upon request. In addition, to run the full-featured TIPSem system, an external tool for semantic role labeling has to be set up and integrated so that using TIPSemB is much more convenient. Thus, and because only the TIPSemB models are directly available, we also use TIPSemB for evaluations and report TIPSemB evaluation results when comparing the quality of the different temporal taggers.

5.2.2   HEIDELTIME—RULE-BASED, MULTILINGUAL, DOMAIN-SENSITIVE

HeidelTime, developed at Heidelberg University, is the first multilingual and domain-sensitive temporal tagger for the full task of temporal tagging. It performs the extraction and the normalization subtasks in a rule-based manner with a rule syntax directly covering both extraction and normalization components [Strötgen and Gertz, 2013]. While HeidelTime was initially developed for processing English news documents [Strötgen and Gertz, 2010], it was shortly after extended to process news- and narrative-style documents with domain-sensitive normalization strategies [Strötgen et al., 2010]. Then, capabilities for processing further languages have been added [Strötgen and Gertz, 2011], and two more domains have been addressed for English colloquial and autonomic (scientific) texts using the Time4SMS and Time4SCI corpora [Strötgen and Gertz, 2012b].

Due to HeidelTime's strict separation of its source code and language-dependent resources, its language resources can be adapted easily. It has been extended by several researchers to further languages and currently covers manually crafted language resources for 13 languages. As will be further detailed in Section 5.5, in addition to the manually created resources for 13 languages, it has recently been automatically extended to more than 200 languages [Strötgen and Gertz, 2015]. Obviously, HeidelTime does not perform equally good for all languages but since most of the languages have never been addressed in the context of temporal tagging, HeidelTime can be used as a baseline temporal tagger or starting point for more than 200 languages.

---

[2]TIPSem implementation without models https://github.com/hllorens/otip [last accessed: Jan 4, 2016]; TIPSemB ready to use library http://gplsi.dlsi.ua.es/demos/TIMEE/ [last accessed: Jan 4, 2016].

In several research competitions, HeidelTime achieved the best evaluation results for the full task of temporal tagging for different languages, namely in TempEval-2 (English) [Verhagen et al., 2010], TempEval-3 (English, Spanish) [UzZaman et al., 2013], and EVALITA'14 (Italian) [Caselli et al., 2014]. It is evaluated on a wide range of temporally annotated corpora including the WikiWars corpus and shows high extraction and normalization quality across languages and domains.[3]

HeidelTime is publicly available as a UIMA component and as a Java standalone version.[4] In addition, it is now also part of GATE-Time [Derczynski et al., 2016], a plugin for the GATE framework.[5] HeidelTime is licensed under the GNU GPL license. The UIMA heideltime-kit also contains several further UIMA components, for example, to read and write annotations in the formats required to perform evaluations with all the corpora developed in the context of the research competitions described in Section 3.3. A further part of HeidelTime is a component to annotate intervals that are not defined in TimeML but valuable for several applications. Such intervals are assigned normalization information in the form of a four-tuple consisting of earliest begin, latest begin, earliest end, and latest end information. For instance, the expression *"between July 2001 and March 2002"* is normalized to ⟨2001-07-01,2001-07-31,2002-03-01,2002-03-31⟩.

Besides its good performance in several evaluation campaigns, two advantages of Heidel-Time are its domain-sensitivity and that it is the only temporal tagger for several languages. In general, HeidelTime is popular and frequently used.[6]

5.2.3 SUTIME—RULE-BASED, STANFORD CORENLP COMPONENT

SUTime was developed by Chang and Manning [2012] at Stanford University and is part of the Stanford CoreNLP package. As HeidelTime, it is a deterministic rule-based system outputting annotations according to the TimeML format (i.e., TIMEX3 annotations), but intervals, not specified in TimeML, can also be annotated. Similar to HeidelTime, the main advantage of rule-based systems is exploited: SUTime is developed with extensibility in mind, for example, rules can be added in a simple way. In contrast to HeidelTime, SUTime supports only the normalization strategy as required when processing news-style documents, that is, the document creation time is used to normalize relative and underspecified temporal expressions. English is so far the only supported language.

The system was developed using the TempEval-2 training data and tested on the TempEval-2 test data. Since it was developed after the competition, it was obviously not evaluated in the context of the TempEval-2 competition. However, SUTime was one of the systems participating in the TempEval-3 competition, where it achieved the best results for relaxed extrac-

---

[3]Overview of HeidelTime's evaluation results, `https://github.com/HeidelTime/heideltime/wiki/Evaluation-Resu lts` [last accessed: Jan 4, 2016].

[4]HeidelTime, `https://github.com/HeidelTime/heideltime/` [last accessed: Jan 4, 2016].

[5]GATE-Time, `https://gate.ac.uk/gate/doc/plugins.html#Tagger_GATE-Time` [last accessed: May 30, 2016].

[6]The two main HeidelTime papers [Strötgen and Gertz, 2010, 2013] have both more than 100 citations according to Google Scholar `https://scholar.google.com/` [last accessed: June 10, 2016]. Although this is not identical to the number of users, it shows HeidelTime's popularity.

tion (English) [Chang and Manning, 2013, UzZaman et al., 2013]. In the full task of temporal tagging, SUTime was outperformed by some systems including HeidelTime.

SUTime is available as Java library and released under the GNU GPL license. A major advantage of SUTime is its integration into the Stanford CoreNLP package. In general, as HeidelTime, SUTime is popular and frequently used.[7]

5.2.4   UWTIME—SEMANTIC PARSING OF TIME EXPRESSIONS

At the University of Washington, Lee et al. [2014] developed the UWTime system, a temporal tagger that uses a semantic parsing approach and applies different normalization strategies for news- and narrative-style documents. In contrast to TIPSem and SUTime, it is thus a domain-sensitive temporal tagger, and next to HeidelTime the second system described here that makes use of domain-sensitive settings.

Lee et al. [2014] aim at a hybrid approach due to the following reasons. First, rule-based systems provide a natural way to express expert knowledge and allow to take into account surrounding linguistic context. Second, machine-learning methods allow to encode preferences between similar competing hypotheses and provide prediction confidence. UWTime combines rule-based and machine-learning methods and uses a Combinatory Categorial Grammar to extract and normalize temporal expressions. As in rule-based systems, the lexicon and the grammar to extract and normalize temporal expressions are manually created. However, the grammar may contain conflicting parses for both, the extraction and the normalization. Thus, a binary classifier is used to resolve conflicts between overlapping expressions and to prune the set of extracted expressions by removing ambiguous phrases, which are determined to not be temporal expressions in the respective contexts. In addition, a log-linear model is used to select the most likely meaning for each temporal expression, that is, the most likely parse of all possible parses is selected. The models are trained separately for processing news- and narrative-style documents to make context-dependent decisions. For the news domain, the TempEval-3 training data is used[8] and for the narrative domain, large parts of the WikiWars corpus. In addition, UWTime can be used with the domain being set to "other". However, no information is provided how the model is trained.

In their evaluation of UWTime, Lee et al. [2014] report very good results on the TempEval-3 test data and the held out part of the WikiWars corpus. Further evaluation details will be provided in the next section. UWTime is publicly available[9] and can be used as standalone tool, rest server, or Java library.

---

[7]The main SUTime paper [Chang and Manning, 2012] has more than 100 citations according to Google Scholar `https://scholar.google.com/` [last accessed: May 15, 2016]. Although this is not identical to the number of users, it shows SUTime's popularity.

[8]Lee et al. [2014] report that they manually corrected the annotations of 18% of the training data due to inconsistencies.

[9]UWTime `https://bitbucket.org/kentonl/uwtime-standalone` [last accessed: Jan 6, 2016].

5.2.5   COMPARISON AND EVALUATION RESULTS

In Table 5.1, we summarize some of the characteristics of the four temporal taggers presented above. Two of the systems (HeidelTime and SUTime) are rule-based and can be easily extended, for example, by adding rules that cover further temporal expressions. In contrast, TIPSem uses a machine learning classifier (conditional random fields) for the extraction and is thus more difficult to adapt. Additional manually annotated data could be used to retrain the model. UWTime follows a hybrid strategy as it relies on a manually developed grammar for the extraction and the normalization, but machine learning is performed to improve the results in order to get rid of spurious temporal expressions and to be able to decide between competing normalizations. While the extension of the grammar is possible, the machine learning models should be retrained after the grammar is modified.

While TIPSem supports English and Spanish, SUTime and UWTime only address processing of English so far. In contrast, HeidelTime is highly multilingual and contains high quality manually created language resources for 13 languages and automatically created language resources for more than 200 languages. With respect to the supported domains, UWTime and HeidelTime both support normalization strategies for news- and narrative-style documents. TIPSem and SUTime, however, do not distinguish between documents of different domains. In addition, HeidelTime supports normalization strategies for colloquial and autonomic-style documents, and also extended language resources for English-colloquial and English-scientific, covering additional vocabulary that is not part of standard English.

The licenses of all four systems are rather restrictive, either GNU GPL or restricted to non-commercial use. In addition, TIPSem and HeidelTime require further tools for linguistic preprocessing, which come with further licenses. Note, however, that the tools listed as further requirements in Table 5.1 are the default tools for preprocessing the respective languages, and that it might be possible to replace them by other tools performing the same tasks. For instance, when HeidelTime is used as a UIMA component, the UIMA heideltime-kit contains several preprocessing wrappers and further preprocessing tools can easily be integrated into the pipeline. It is important that the same types of annotations are produced and that the same tagset for part-of-speech tagging is used.

As the Stanford CoreNLP package contains components to perform linguistic preprocessing, no further tools are required to use SUTime. Similarly, necessary components for preprocessing are also part of UWTime, namely components of the University of Washington Semantic Parsing Framework (UW SPF).

If licensing is an issue, the ClearTK-TimeML system described below might be an alternative as its license is less restrictive. Although it does not natively support the normalization of temporal expressions, it can be combined with tools for normalization, as will be detailed below.

Table 5.1: Comparison of the temporal taggers TIPSem, HeidelTime, SUTime, and UWTime (*Continues.*)

	TIPSem(B)	HeidelTime	SUTime	UWTime
Extraction	CRFs	Rules	Rules	Hybrid
Normalization	Rules	Rules	Rules	Hybrid
Domains	News	News, narrative, colloquial*, autonomic*	News	News, narrative
Languages	2 English, Spanish	13 (plus >200) Arabic, Chinese, Croatian, Dutch, English, Estonian, French, German, Italian, Portuguese, Russian, Spanish, Vietnamese, more than 200 "auto-languages"	1 English	1 English
Licence	Research, education	GNU GPL	GNU GPL	GNU GPL
Further required tools	TreeTagger[1] FreeLing[2]	TreeTagger[3] Stanford Tagger[4] HunPos Tagger[5] JVnTextPro[6] none[7]	none[8]	none[9]

*Although HeidelTime contains normalization strategies for colloquial and autonomic in general, both also rely on additional vocabulary which is only available for English.

Table 5.1: (*Continued.*) Comparison of the temporal taggers TIPSem, HeidelTime, SUTime, and UWTime

[1]for English: TreeTagger [Schmid, 1994],

[2]for Spanish: FreeLing http://nlp.lsi.upc.edu/freeling/ [last accessed: Jan 6, 2016],

[3]for Chinese, Dutch, English, Estonian, French, German, Italian, Portuguese, Russian, Spanish: TreeTagger [Schmid, 1994],

[4]for Arabic: Stanford POS tagger [Toutanova et al., 2003],

[5]for Croatian: HunPos Tagger [Halácsy et al., 2007],

[6]for Vietnamese: JVnTextPro [Nguyen et al., 2010],

[7]for auto-languages: no external tool required, generic preprocessing is part of HeidelTime,

[8]no external tool required as SUTime is part of Stanford CoreNLP http://nlp.stanford.edu/software/corenlp.shtml [last accessed: Jan 6, 2016],

[9]no external tool required as UWTime contains necessary semantic parsing components of the UW Semantic Parsing Framework [Artzi and Zettlemoyer, 2013].

TEMPEVAL-3 COMPETITION RESULTS FOR ENGLISH TEMPORAL TAGGING

Three of the described tools (TIPSem, HeidelTime, SUTime) have been evaluated in the context of the TempEval-3 competition for the English temporal tagging task, in which the training and test data consist of news documents (cf. Section 3.3, page 32 and Section 3.4, page 39). Note that TIPSem was evaluated but not TIPSemB, and that TIPSem is the system of one of the organizers of the shared task so that its results were listed separately.

In Table 5.2, we list the official evaluation results as reported by the TempEval-3 organizers [UzZaman et al., 2013]. For the extraction subtask, precision, recall, and f1-score are reported for relaxed matching and f1-score for strict matching. For the full task of temporal tagging, the value f1 measure is reported, which combines relaxed matching with correct value normalization (cf. Section 3.2, page 25, for details about evaluation measures).

The three HeidelTime results correspond to different versions of the system [Strötgen et al., 2013]. While HeidelTime 1.2 was the publicly available version before the TempEval-3 challenge took place, HeidelTime-bf is a bug-fixed version in which minor modifications have been realized independent of the TempEval-3 competition. Finally, HeidelTime-t is the version that was tuned for TempEval-3, in particular to better handle ambiguous expressions. HeidelTime-t corresponds to the publicly released HeidelTime version 1.3. SUTime and TIPSem were not modified for the TempEval-3 competition.

The evaluation results in Table 5.2 reveal that TIPSem achieved the highest f1-score of the three systems for strict matching.[10] Furthermore, for relaxed matching, TIPSem reaches the highest precision, SUTime the highest recall, and SUTime and HeidelTime almost identical f1-

---

[10]Note that another system—ClearTK-TimeML [Bethard, 2013b]—achieved a slightly higher f1-score for strict matching (82.7%). For details on ClearTK-TimeML, see Section 5.4, page 100.

Table 5.2: The official English TempEval-3 results of three HeidelTime versions, SUTime, and TIPSem as reported by the organizers [UzZaman et al., 2013]

	p	r	f1	strict f1	value f1
HeidelTime-t	93.08	87.68	90.30	81.34	77.61
HeidelTime-bf	90.00	84.78	87.31	78.36	72.39
HeidelTime 1.2	89.31	84.78	86.99	78.07	72.12
SUTime	89.36	91.30	90.32	79.57	67.38
TIPSem	97.20	75.36	84.90	81.63	65.31

Table 5.3: The official Spanish TempEval-3 results of HeidelTime and TIPSemB as reported by the organizers [UzZaman et al., 2013]

	p	r	f1	strict f1	value f1
HeidelTime	96.02	84.92	90.13	85.33	85.33
TIPSemB	93.68	81.91	87.40	82.57	71.85

scores with SUTime's f1-score being 0.02 percentage points higher than HeidelTime's f1-score. For the full task of temporal tagging, that is, for relaxed extraction with correct normalization (value f1), all three HeidelTime versions outperformed all other participants' systems including SUTime and TIPSem, and HeidelTime-t significantly increased HeidelTime's value f1-score.

TEMPEVAL-3 COMPETITION RESULTS FOR SPANISH TEMPORAL TAGGING

Two of the described systems (TIPSem, HeidelTime) have also been evaluated for Spanish temporal tagging at TempEval-3, that is, on Spanish news documents. Note that for Spanish, TIPSemB results and not TIPSem results are reported by UzZaman et al. [2013]. In Table 5.3, TIPSemB's and HeidelTime's official evaluation results are shown.[11]

Both systems, TIPSemB—which was the best performing system for Spanish temporal tagging at the TempEval-2 competition—and HeidelTime achieve very good results for the extraction of temporal expressions, although HeidelTime achieves better results for both, relaxed and strict matching. For the full task (value f1), HeidelTime clearly outperforms TIPSemB.

FURTHER TEMPEVAL-3 RESULTS

UWTime was developed after the TempEval-3 competition and also evaluated on the TempEval-3 test data, which was held out during its development. In addition, further HeidelTime versions

---

[11]Note that in their TempEval-3 task description paper, UzZaman et al. [2013] accidentally reported type f1 numbers as scores for value f1 for the Spanish results. In Table 5.3, the actual value f1 scores are listed.

Table 5.4: Evaluation results of UWTime and HeidelTime 2.0 on the English TempEval-3 test data reported after the competition, as well as the official TempEval-3 results (lower part)

	p	r	f1	strict f1	value f1
UWTime	94.6	88.4	91.4	83.1	82.4
HeidelTime (v. 2.0)	93.1	88.4	90.7	81.8	78.1
HeidelTime-t	93.08	87.68	90.30	81.34	77.61
HeidelTime-bf	90.00	84.78	87.31	78.36	72.39
HeidelTime 1.2	89.31	84.78	86.99	78.07	72.12
SUTime	89.36	91.30	90.32	79.57	67.38
TIPSem	97.20	75.36	84.90	81.63	65.31

were released. In Table 5.4, we report UWTime's evaluation results as reported by Lee et al. [2014] and the results of HeidelTime's current version 2.0.

UWTime outperforms HeidelTime's TempEval-3 and 2.0 versions on the English TempEval-3 test data, and therefore all systems of the TempEval-3 participants. It currently achieves the best reported temporal tagging results on the TempEval-3 test data set.

EVALUATIONS ON THE NARRATIVE CORPUS WIKIWARS

For the development and evaluation of UWTime, Lee et al. [2014] split the narrative corpus WikiWars into a training set and a test set with 17 and 5 documents, respectively. That is, UW-Time was developed on large parts of WikiWars. In contrast, except of two documents that are also part of the English AncientTimes corpus (i.e., two documents about historic content), Wiki-Wars was not used to develop HeidelTime but only used for its evaluation.

In Table 5.5, we show UWTime's evaluation results on the two subsets as reported by Lee et al. [2014]. In addition, we show the results of UWTime's and HeidelTime's publicly available versions on the full corpus. Note that there is no official division of WikiWars into a training set and a test set, and no information about which documents belong to which set is available. Thus, we cannot provide HeidelTime's results on the two sets separately.

Lee et al. [2014] also reported HeidelTime's performance on their two WikiWars subsets. However, they used a HeidelTime version that did not cover historic temporal expressions, because the extension of HeidelTime to a version that also detects historic temporal expressions (version 1.7, released in May 2014) [Strötgen et al., 2014b] and UWTime's development temporally overlapped. While UWTime outperformed the old HeidelTime version, Table 5.5 indicates that the latest HeidelTime version performs pretty much as well as UWTime on the WikiWars corpus.

Table 5.5: UWTime's results on two sets of the WikiWars corpus that were used for development and evaluation as reported by Lee et al. [2014], and results of UWTime's and HeidelTime's publicly available versions on the full WikiWars corpus

	p	r	f1	strict f1	value f1
UWTime (training set)	98.1	90.1	93.9	86.5	82.3
UWTime (test set)	97.6	87.6	92.3	80.3	78.1
UWTime (full corpus)	99.2	87.3	92.9	88.1	83.3
HeidelTime 2.0 (full corpus)	98.3	86.0	91.7	87.0	83.0

EVALUATIONS ON CORPORA OF FURTHER LANGUAGES

As HeidelTime is the only one of the four described systems that can process several further languages, we do not report evaluation results for other languages, but refer to the HeidelTime web page where its evaluation results on publicly available corpora of many languages are reported.[12]

HeidelTime and UWTime support domain-sensitive temporal tagging, and SUTime and TIPSem do not distinguish between documents of different domains. To show the importance of domain-sensitive temporal tagging, in the next section, we present the evaluation results of the four systems on non-news corpora.

5.3 THE VALUE OF DOMAIN-SENSITIVE TEMPORAL TAGGING

While the evaluation results of the four temporal taggers on news documents and UWTime's and HeidelTime's evaluation results on the WikiWars corpus already show that high quality temporal tagging performance on news and narrative documents is possible, the necessity of domain-sensitive temporal tagging was not yet proven. To demonstrate the value of domain-sensitive temporal tagging, we ran the four temporal taggers with all their settings for different domains (if applicable) on the corpora of the four different domains, which we used in our comparative corpus analysis in Section 4.5 (TimeBank, WikiWars, Time4SMS, Time4SCI). The results are shown in Table 5.6.[13] Note that we ignore that (parts of) some corpora have been used to develop the systems. Thus, the results are not directly comparable. However, they clearly show the value of domain-sensitive temporal tagging.

The results clearly indicate that all four taggers can achieve good evaluation results on the news corpus (TimeBank), but for UWTime and HeidelTime, it is important that the settings for

---

[12]https://github.com/HeidelTime/heideltime/wiki/Evaluation-Results [last accessed: Jan 6, 2016].

[13]We performed some simple TIMEX2-TIMEX3 value conversions to make sure that correct system annotations are evaluated as correct on the TIMEX2 corpora. In addition, some of the corpora contain special characters that were partially replaced by the systems and lead to offset issues during the evaluation. We manually checked the evaluation results of the systems and corrected these issues. However, rerunning the experiments using the publicly available corpora and evaluation scripts will thus result in (slightly) different numbers.

Table 5.6: Evaluating HeidelTime (version 2.0), UWTime, SUTime, and TIPSemB on corpora of four different domains (using relaxed f1 and relaxed value f1 measures); HeidelTime and UWTime are used with all domain-sensitive settings; results on domains for which systems were particularly developed are highlighted; results are calculated without considering DCTs

	TimeBank[1] News		WikiWars Narrative		Time4SMS Colloquial		Time4SCI Scientific	
	f1 (relaxed)	value f1	f1 (relaxed)	value f1	f1 (relaxed)	value f1	f1 (relaxed)	value f1
HeidelTime								
• News	**91.9**	**79.6**	91.7	60.8	57.5	48.3	68.5	46.0
• Narrative	91.9	29.3	**91.7**	**83.0**	57.5	40.3	68.5	46.0
• Colloquial	90.5	78.0	87.9	55.5	**79.1**	**66.9**	71.3	49.5
• Scientific	90.6	72.9	87.9	55.1	59.6	51.0	**77.4**	**66.4**
UWTime								
• News	**94.6**	**82.4**	91.8	60.1	57.5	42.3	71.0	31.7
• Narrative	83.7	45.8	**92.9**	**83.3**	58.1	35.9	62.9	37.1
• Other	93.3	80.6	92.0	79.8	55.8	44.8	71.0	34.4
SUTime[2]	**90.9**	**70.3**	91.0	49.9	72.2	56.0	76.2	34.5
TIPSemB	**99.4**	**73.7**	71.1	39.6	37.3	22.1	41.4	19.0

[1]The slightly improved TempEval-3 version of TimeBank was used (cf. Section 3.4, page 38).
[2]Used with `restrictToTimex3 = true` as suggested by Chang and Manning [2013].

processing news documents are selected. UWTime and HeidelTime also achieve very good results on the WikiWars corpus for the extraction and the normalization when applied with their settings for processing narratives. In contrast, TIPSemB and SUTime—as HeidelTime and UWTime with their news strategies—fail to correctly normalize many temporal expressions. For instance, HeidelTime's value f1 score can be boosted from 60.8% to 83.0% when processing WikiWars with HeidelTime's narrative normalization strategy instead of its normalization strategy for processing news. While SUTime still achieves high extraction results and rather low normalization results, TIPSemB performs worse for both the extraction and the normalization. The rather low extraction quality is probably mainly, because we had to use TIPSemB in the evaluation, that is, TIPSem without its semantic features, which proved to be helpful in generalizing (cf. Section 5.2.1).

Processing WikiWars as news-style documents with the four systems results in the best value f1 score of 60.8% in contrast to the best value f1 score of 83.3% that was achieved when processing WikiWars as narrative documents. Similarly, processing TimeBank as narrative-style documents with HeidelTime and UWTime results in very low value f1 scores. These findings clearly show the importance of tackling news- and narrative-style documents differently, that is, that domain-sensitive temporal tagging is required.

HeidelTime also offers normalization strategies for processing colloquial and autonomic-style documents and therefore contains specific English-colloquial and English-scientific language resources. Thus, the characteristics of colloquial and scientific documents can be tackled quite successfully. It is not surprising that on the Time4SCI corpus, HeidelTime with its news, narrative, and colloquial settings—exactly as UWTime, SUTime, and TIPSem—fails to normalize many of the temporal expressions. This is because the corpus contains several annotations that can only be resolved with respect to a local time frame, that is, not according to the original TimeML specifications (cf. Section 4.3, page 51). In contrast, Time4SMS only contains TimeML-compliant annotations and the results in Table 5.6 show that temporal taggers developed for processing news- or narrative-style documents tend to miss several expressions occurring in colloquial documents, which results in lower extraction and normalization quality.

In general, the results in Table 5.6 demonstrate how important it is to tackle domain-dependent challenges when temporal tagging of documents of different domains. The autonomic domain (e.g., scientific documents) will require further attention in the future. In contrast, the domain of colloquial-style documents might be considered as a rather narrow domain, and its difficulties can be quite successfully tackled as it was described in Section 4.4.3 (page 61). This is also shown by the results of HeidelTime with its colloquial settings. As the results of HeidelTime and UWTime demonstrate, the differences between news- and narrative-style documents can and should be addressed by applying domain-dependent normalization strategies.

5.4 APPROACHES TO SUBTASKS AND RELATED TASKS

Besides full-fledged temporal taggers, there have been several approaches addressing only subtasks of temporal tagging or closely related tasks. In the following, we briefly describe ClearTK-TimeML as a tool for the extraction subtask, some approaches to the normalization subtask, and DCTFinder for the detection of document creation times.

CLEARTK—ML-BASED EXTRACTION AND CLASSIFICATION

ClearTK [Bethard et al., 2014, Ogren et al., 2008] from the University of Colorado at Boulder is a UIMA-based framework to develop statistical natural language processing components. In the context of TempEval-3, ClearTK-TimeML was developed to perform the full task of English temporal annotation [Bethard, 2013b]. It is realized as a pipeline of machine-learning models. For temporal tagging, the extraction and classification subtasks are modeled as a IOB token-chunking task and multi-class classification, respectively, each making use of simple morpho-syntactic features and a small gazetteer of time words. The normalization of temporal expressions was not addressed but the time normalization tool TIMEN described below was used. Different machine learning classifiers (CRF, SVM, logistic regression for the extraction, SVM and maximum entropy for the classification) were tested with several parameter settings on the TempEval-3 training data, and the best model-parameter combinations were selected for the TempEval-3 submission.

In addition to a very good overall performance in TempEval-3, ClearTK-TimeML performed the best for strict extraction of temporal expressions (English) [Bethard, 2013b, UzZaman et al., 2013]. For the full task of temporal tagging, ClearTK-TimeML—that is, ClearTK-TimeML's extraction model with TIMEN for normalization—was outperformed by some systems including SUTime and HeidelTime.

ClearTK including ClearTK-TimeML is publicly available.[14] While ClearTK-TimeML is not a full temporal tagger, it can be combined with tools performing the normalization subtasks only. These are briefly described next.

APPROACHES TO THE NORMALIZATION SUBTASK

Recently, a couple of approaches have been developed to perform the task of normalizing temporal expressions independently of the extraction. TIMEN [Llorens et al., 2012a] was the first normalization-only tool. It is a rule-based system that requires the expression itself as input. Furthermore, it requires the document creation time, information about the reference time, and the tense of the sentence. Since the detection of the correct reference time (and also the detection of the tense) is one of the difficult parts during the normalization phase (and, in addition, domain-dependent as was detailed in Chapter 4) it is not sufficient to just perform the extraction subtask before applying TIMEN for the normalization. Although TIMEN aimed at becoming a community-driven tool for the normalization subtask of temporal tagging and is still publicly available, it is rarely used anymore.[15]

Three further approaches to perform only the normalization task of temporal tagging have been developed by Angeli et al. [2012], Angeli and Uszkoreit [2013], and Bethard [2013a]. All three approaches run a parsing strategy to normalize temporal expressions and were approaches that motivated the development of UWTime as a full temporal tagger for parsing temporal expressions. While Bethard [2013a] manually developed the parsing grammar, the approaches by Angeli et al. [2012] and Angeli and Uszkoreit [2013] present the first approaches to learn the task of normalization. However, of the three tools, only the system developed by Bethard [2013a] is publicly available.[16] In addition, it has been extended to Italian [Mirza and Minard, 2014] and Indonesian [Mirza, 2015].[17]

Note that using separate tools for the extraction and the normalization of temporal expressions results in difficulties, in particular if the goal is to perform temporal tagging of documents of

---

[14]ClearTK `https://github.com/ClearTK/cleartk` [last accessed: Jan 6, 2016].
[15]TIMEN `https://code.google.com/p/timen/` [last accessed: Jan 6, 2016].
[16]Timenorm `https://github.com/bethard/timenorm/` [last accessed: Jan 6, 2016].
[17]Timenorm for Italian: `https://github.com/paramitamirza/timennorm` [last accessed: May 15, 2016];
  Timenorm for Indonesian: `https://github.com/paramitamirza/IndoTimex` [last accessed: May 15, 2016].

different domains because the main challenges remain. For example, extraction-only tools do not provide information about what the correct reference time is (e.g., the reference time of relative and underspecified expressions). However, normalization-only tools do not distinguish between domains, so that this information would be required as input. Thus, we do not go into any detail and do not provide evaluation results of these approaches.

DCTFINDER—DETECTING DOCUMENT CREATION TIMES

So far, we have assumed that a document is either from the news, narrative, colloquial, or autonomic domain. In addition, if a document is from the news or colloquial domain, we expect that a document creation time (DCT) is provided together with the document's text that is to be processed by the temporal tagger. This is reasonable because the DCT plays a crucial role for the normalization of underspecified and relative temporal expressions on these domains. However, well formatted document collections containing the DCT as easily accessible metadata such as the New York Times corpus[18]—despite being used frequently in research scenarios—are not typical when the goal is to process more heterogeneous types of text data. A lot of content is published on the Web, and well-formatted web pages that include metadata (DCTs) are rather an exception.

As it is difficult to correctly extract the titles, content, and, in particular, the DCTs of web pages, the detection of the document creation times of web pages is an important side topic of temporal tagging. Without the document creation time, underspecified and relative temporal expressions cannot be normalized correctly if the web pages contain news-style content. This is particularly problematic, because such expressions are very frequent in news documents, as we showed in our comparative corpus analysis (cf. Figure 4.12, page 73).

A recently developed system aiming at detecting the DCTs of news web pages is DCTFinder [Tannier, 2014]. A good hint that a date might be the DCT is its textual proximity to the document's title. Thus, DCTFinder first relies on some heuristics to extract a document's title. In a second step, DCTFinder aims at detecting the DCT of a web page. However, often web pages contain the document creation time, the current time, and the last modified time. These are rather difficult to differentiate, because they occur in very similar contexts. Thus, a CRF classifier is applied that aims at extracting all three types of dates. For this, several lexical features (e.g., whether a token is in a time word gazetteer) and structural features (e.g., the number of dates occurring before the token, distance to the title) are used to learn a CRF model, which returns a list of DCT candidates. These are then normalized in a straightforward way by replacing month names by respective numbers etc. While the three types of document-related dates are difficult to distinguish, once they are normalized, the DCT can easily be determined as it is simply the earliest date.

---

[18]The New York Times corpus is frequently used as a data set, e.g., in the context of temporal information retrieval. It contains over 1.8 million well formatted news documents of the *New York Times* from the years 1987–2007 and it is released by the Linguistic Data Consortium. https://catalog.ldc.upenn.edu/LDC2008T19 [last accessed: Jan 6, 2016].

For training the classifier and for evaluating DCTFinder, Tannier [2014] manually annotated two English and a French collection of news web pages. While one of the English data sets is used to train the model using ten-fold cross validation, the other two data sets are only used for evaluation purposes. The results of 87% to over 92% accuracy show that DCTFinder can be used in real-world applications to detect the DCT of news web pages. The evaluation also shows that the results are similarly good on the French data set although the model was learned on English annotated data only. As a major challenge, the distinction between U.S. and UK style dates is mentioned, for example, 04/02/2015 typically refers to the second of April and to the fourth of February on U.S. and UK web pages, respectively. This is one difficulty that is in general a challenge for temporal taggers as we will also point out in Chapter 6.

DCTFinder with accompanying data and models is publicly available.[19]

5.5   HIGHLY MULTILINGUAL TEMPORAL TAGGING

Temporal taggers are usually developed for a certain language, and rule-based systems are sometimes manually extended to further languages. For instance, two of the temporal taggers detailed above are multilingual systems: TIPSem (and TIPSemB) can process English and Spanish, and HeidelTime contains manually created language resources for 13 languages (HeidelTime version 2.0). Due to HeidelTime's strict separation between language resources and the source code and due to its well-defined rule syntax, it was possible that several researchers at different institutes developed HeidelTime language resources.[20]

AUTOMATIC APPROACHES TO MULTILINGUALITY

While the advantage of manually extending a temporal tagger to additional languages is that no training data is required, such extensions are quite time- and labor-intensive. Thus, there have also been approaches to perform the extension to a target language (semi-)automatically [Negri et al., 2006, Saquete et al., 2004, Spreyer and Frank, 2008]. However, these early approaches were limited to a few languages, and the results were considered less successful, in particular for the normalization subtask. In contrast, Angeli and Uszkoreit [2013] presented an approach to language-independent parsing of temporal expressions. However, they only addressed the normalization and not the extraction of temporal expressions, and experiments were only performed on news-style data.

---

[19]DCTFinder http://sourceforge.net/p/dctfinder/ [last accessed: Jan 6, 2016].
[20]Several researchers developed resources for the 13 languages contained in HeidelTime version 2.0 at Heidelberg University (Arabic [Strötgen et al., 2014a], Chinese [Li et al., 2014], English [Strötgen and Gertz, 2013], Estonian, German [Strötgen and Gertz, 2011], Italian [Manfredi et al., 2014], Spanish [Strötgen et al., 2013], Vietnamese [Strötgen et al., 2014a]), University of Zagreb (Croatian [Skukan et al., 2014]), Tilburg University (Dutch [van de Camp and Christiansen, 2012]), LIMSI (French [Moriceau and Tannier, 2014]), Moscow National Research University Higher School Of Economics (Russian), and CACI Inc. (Portuguese).

AUTOMATIC APPROACH TO ADDRESS ALL LANGUAGES

More recently, the automatic extension of a temporal tagger was re-addressed aiming at a HeidelTime extension that covers the extraction and the normalization of temporal expressions in all languages of the world [Strötgen and Gertz, 2015]. Based on the experiences the developers gained from manual extensions [e.g., Li et al., 2014, Skukan et al., 2014, Strötgen et al., 2014a], a module was developed to automatically create language resources for HeidelTime for more than 200 languages. For this, the original English resources were simplified to make them amenable to automatic translation. Since linguistic preprocessing was reduced to sentence splitting and tokenization in order to avoid language-dependent part-of-speech tagging, the rules do not contain any part-of-speech information.

For translating the English patterns, all their translations listed on Wiktionary[21] were collected for all available languages. In addition, the rules were written in a language-independent way, that is, they only refer to the abstract names of the pattern lists (e.g., names of months, weekdays, etc.) and do not contain any words directly. Thus, the same rules can be applied for all languages. During processing documents of a specific language, HeidelTime automatically replaces the abstract pattern names in the rules with the patterns of the respective language. In addition, the rules are designed in such a way that they aim at a rather flexible matching of temporal expressions. For instance, they cover word order permutations of multi-term temporal expressions that may be valid in some languages but do not occur in others. The assumption is that some rules will not match any temporal expression in some of the languages but are useful for other languages. However, even if a rule does not match any temporal expression in a specific language, this rule will also not harm the extraction quality, because it does not match other phrases.

The manual development process of the simplified English resources and the language-independent rules have been carried out using only HeidelTime's original English resources and English temporally annotated corpora. Thus, no data about the target languages are required except for the translations in Wiktionary. Furthermore, none of the temporally annotated non-English corpora (cf. Section 3.4 and Section 4.3) has been used during the development so that all the corpora were applicable to evaluate the extraction and normalization quality of HeidelTime's automatically created resources.

In Table 5.7, we show the comparison of the extraction and normalization quality of HeidelTime with automatically developed resources and the quality of HeidelTime with manually developed resources.[22] While the results with the automatically developed resources are worse than those with the manually developed resources, promising results have been achieved in many languages. There are still several open issues, for instance, how to deal with languages without whitespace token boundaries, but in particular with respect to the precision and normalization quality the results are encouraging. For most reported languages, the automatically developed resources miss many expressions (i.e., low recall in general, very low recall for some languages,

---

[21]Wiktionary, `https://www.wiktionary.com/` [last accessed: May 15, 2016].
[22]For more details about evaluation results and results for further languages see [Strötgen and Gertz, 2015].

Table 5.7: Comparison of HeidelTime's manually developed resources and automatically created resources for some languages as reported by Strötgen and Gertz [2015]

Language (corpus)	HeidelTime (manual)					HeidelTime (automatic)				
	Relaxed Extr.			Value		Relaxed Extr.			Value	
	p	r	f1	f1	acc	p	r	f1	f1	acc
Arabic (Arabic test-50*)	90.9	90.9	90.9	82.2	90.4	91.7	31.8	47.2	38.0	80.5
Croatian (WikiWarsHR)	92.6	90.5	91.5	80.8	88.3	87.3	6.8	12.6	9.7	77.0
French (FR-TimeBank)	91.9	90.1	91.0	73.6	80.9	87.2	59.5	70.8	54.6	77.1
Portuguese (PT-TimeBank Test)	87.3	75.9	81.2	63.5	78.2	91.5	59.3	72.0	59.4	82.5
Spanish (TempEval-3 Test)	96.0	84.9	90.1	85.3	94.7	95.5	53.8	68.8	58.5	85.0

e.g., Croatian), but extracted expressions are often normalized correctly (i.e., high precision, high value accuracy). Also note that an evaluation could only be performed for those languages for which temporally annotated corpora were available.

Since HeidelTime with language resources for more than 200 languages is publicly available, it can either be used as a baseline for temporal tagging of many languages or as a starting point for further developments. In particular because temporal tagging is now possible for a wide range of languages for which no temporal tagger has been available before, we expect that this will boost both, further research on temporal tagging of languages not addressed before, and applications exploiting temporal information.

5.6   SUMMARY OF THE CHAPTER

In this chapter, we gave an overview of tools and techniques for temporal tagging. These range from rule-based and machine-learning systems to hybrid and parsing approaches. While a lot of research on temporal tagging focused on temporal tagging of English news-style documents, more recently, more and more languages were tackled and the differences between documents of different domains were addressed. With detailed descriptions of four publicly available temporal taggers, we presented the current state-of-the-art in temporal tagging. While TIPSem(B) and SUTime are two temporal taggers that do not distinguish between documents of different domains, UWTime and HeidelTime perform domain-sensitive temporal tagging. An evaluation of the four temporal taggers on corpora of four different domains demonstrated the importance of domain-sensitive temporal tagging. We briefly presented tools addressing only one of the two subtasks (extraction or normalization) and a tool for detecting document creation times on news web pages. Finally, the topic of highly multilingual temporal tagging was described, which is still one of the open issues of temporal tagging as will also be discussed in the next chapter.

CHAPTER 6

Summary and Future Research Directions

6.1 SUMMARY

Temporal tagging covers the extraction and normalization of temporal expressions and is an important subtask in multiple natural language processing and understanding applications. The overwhelming amount of textual data—may it be written from its origin or transcribed spoken data—is tough to understand without the detection and interpretation of the meaning of temporal expressions. For instance, many types of relations in texts could not be detected, many questions could not be answered, many information needs could not be interpreted, many relations between texts within larger collections would be lost, and many summaries might be misunderstood. Thus, temporal tagging is a key component in natural language processing applications, and research on temporal tagging gains more and more interest.

Originally driven by applications in the area of business news analytics, documents of the news domain were the area of focus in temporal tagging research at its beginning—as for most natural language processing tasks in general. However, more recently, more and more work has arisen to tackle the task of temporal tagging when dealing with other types of documents ranging from Wikipedia articles, user-generated social media content, conversations, scientific publications, (bio)medical narratives, and literature. Thus, the originally developed methods for temporal tagging have to be analyzed and validated with respect to their quality for both subtasks (i.e., extraction and normalization) when processing documents of different domains. For some types of documents, extensions of the vocabulary and temporal knowledge about this vocabulary are sufficient. However, some types of documents differ significantly with respect to their characteristics that are relevant for the task of temporal tagging. Whenever identical expressions require domain-dependent strategies for their interpretation, the documents should be clustered into different domains, and temporal taggers should be designed in such a way that they know how to deal with different domains.

In this book, we described the subtasks of temporal tagging (extraction, classification, normalization), surveyed research competitions that tackle this task, and presented annotation standards for temporal expressions. We also discussed temporally annotated corpora of news and non-news documents and explained evaluation scenarios for determining the quality of temporal taggers.

We focused on domain-sensitive temporal tagging by studying the characteristics of temporal expressions, documents, and corpora of different domains, and by suggesting several strategies for how the challenges can be addressed. However, a further important topic besides domain-sensitivity is multilingual temporal tagging. Thus, we included not only English temporally annotated corpora and English-focused research competitions in our survey, but additionally covered works dealing with other languages. Furthermore, we also surveyed publicly available temporal taggers and presented the state-of-the-art in temporal tagging of English and non-English documents of different domains. Finally, we discussed a first work toward highly multilingual temporal tagging, a topic that probably will receive further attention in the research community in the future.

6.2 FUTURE DIRECTIONS

Besides further approaches to multilingual temporal tagging, there are several issues that need to be addressed and that result in interesting research questions. In the following, we formulate several ideas and possible future directions for temporal tagging research.

MULTILINGUAL TEMPORAL TAGGING AND NEVER ADDRESSED LANGUAGES

There are many languages that have never been touched by any research on temporal tagging, except in the context of the fully automatic extension of HeidelTime [Strötgen and Gertz, 2015]. There is a lot of room for work on temporal tagging in specific languages and for work on studying temporal phenomena in different languages. In addition, temporal taggers such as HeidelTime could be extended by researchers with respective language skills to make available manually developed, high quality temporal tagging capacities for many more languages than those that are currently supported.

REFERENCE TIME IDENTIFICATION

An interesting research question is how it is possible to decide whether or not a temporal expression is suitable as a reference time for underspecified and relative temporal expressions. Improvements in this area will not result in huge improvements of the evaluation results of temporal taggers, because simple methods such as using the document creation time or the previously mentioned expression can be used in many cases. Still, it is impossible to achieve more sophisticated temporal tagging output when ignoring this issue. Approaches will have to move toward a better natural language understanding. Better methods to normalize temporal expressions for which a non-standard reference time is required will further increase the popularity of temporal taggers and their usage in other applications.

DEEPER UNDERSTANDING OF LOCAL TIME FRAMES

As a fourth domain, we presented the autonomic domain. All documents with temporal expressions that cannot be normalized to real points in time but only with respect to their own local time frame are part of this domain. While we presented several suggestions on how to deal with temporal expressions in such documents, there is still a lot of work that needs to be done. Besides precise and generally accepted annotation guidelines, it will be important that temporal taggers are aware of the possibility that a document may contain temporal expressions that should not be normalized to real points in time. An analysis of how this can be detected, and methods for how to determine so-called time point zeros for local normalizations are open issues. These have to be addressed in the future when domain-sensitive temporal tagging is the goal.

TOPIC-SPECIFIC ADAPTATIONS

Although a wide range of documents is covered by the four domains introduced in this book, there are still some differences between different types of documents—even if they belong to the same domain. For instance, we already mentioned that in documents about history and in documents about biomedical content, a temporal tagger's vocabulary should be extended to fit the needs of the respective documents. Further examples are: (i) (scientific) documents about geology, in which very long durations ("*3.5 Ma*", i.e., 3.5 megaannum, 3.5 million years) and names referring to time eras (e.g., "*Mesozoic Era*") occur frequently [Leveling, 2015]; (ii) documents about sport events, in which references to specific time points within a game's time frame are referenced (e.g., "*the 2nd minute of the second half*" refers to the 47th minute of the game if the document is about soccer); and (iii) more generally, all types of documents in which other types of calendars are used (e.g., the Hindi Moon Calendar).

For all these examples, the "temporal knowledge" of a temporal tagger would have to be enriched to correctly detect and normalize respective expressions, and it is very likely that topic-specific adaptations (and settings) will be necessary.

AUTOMATIC DOMAIN IDENTIFICATION

So far, temporal taggers that distinguish the processing of different domains require that the user specifies the domain of the documents that are to be processed. However, in particular when processing heterogeneous (web) content, it would be desirable if the choice of the domain was performed automatically on the document level. As we showed in the comparative corpus analysis, the documents of four domains tend to be quite different, for example, there are some temporal expressions that occur frequently in news documents (e.g., today, tomorrow, Monday) but are rare in the other domains. In contrast, narrative texts tend to span a larger time interval and contain many more references to historic dates. All the information about the differences between documents of the different domains could be exploited to develop a model to determine a document's domain.

Obviously, if the automatic domain identification determines a document as a news or colloquial document, sophisticated methods to automatically detect a document's creation time will have to be applied, too. Otherwise, the reference time of many temporal expressions would be unspecified, and there would be no benefit of automatically identifying the domain.

CONFIDENCE INFORMATION

Applications for which a correct extraction of temporal expressions is crucial, or for which it would be better that an expression was not extracted rather than normalized incorrectly, are currently faced with the problem of deciding what expressions should be taken into consideration. For such applications, meaningful confidence scores would be of great value.

However, temporal taggers usually provide no confidence information, although the likelihood that expressions are correctly extracted and normalized varies. For instance, it is obvious that expressions explicitly referring to a particular day ("*January 2, 2015*") are more likely to be normalized correctly than relative ("*next year*") and underspecified expressions ("*January*"), whose meanings depend on context information.

Simply assigning higher confidence scores to explicit expressions than to underspecified and relative expressions would only cover one aspect that influences the likelihood whether expressions are correct. Explicit and underspecified expressions may or may not be ambiguous. For example, "*January 2, 2015*" is rather unambiguous, but it depends on the context whether a four-digit number such as "*2000*" is an explicit temporal expressions (e.g., "In *2000*, we ..." vs. "In *2000* miles, we ..."). Even confidence scores for quite similar expressions that could be extracted based on the same features or with the same rule should be distinct. For example, "*March*" and "*January*" are both names of months, but "*March*" might also be used in different contexts, for example, in phrases such as "*March* of the Iron Will". Such ambiguities should be considered.

Furthermore, even the likelihood of identical expressions is not always equally high but depends on how difficult it is to determine the correct reference time. It might happen that the reference time has to be determined among many temporal expressions or there might be just a single possible reference time. Similarly, the difficulty of determining the correct relation to a reference time (e.g., in absence of tense information or based on tense information) should also influence a confidence score.

TIME ZONES, HEMISPHERES, AND WEAKNESSES IN ANNOTATION STANDARDS

A further issue occurs whenever different time zones come into play. For instance, texts from Twitter often contain temporal expressions of the type "time" and the normalization can often be resolved with respect to the sending time of the message. However, all tweets contain identical sending time information independent of where a tweet was sent. This results in the issue that an expression such as "*9 pm*" in two tweets sent from within the U.S. and from within the UK will receive identical normalized time information, although they do not refer to the same point in time.

A similar issue that is mostly ignored in temporal tagging research are the differences between the northern hemisphere and the southern hemisphere. According to the annotation standards for temporal expressions (TIMEX2 and TIMEX3), the expression *"summer 2003"* is to be normalized to 2003-SU. However, depending on whether one refers to the summer of the northern or southern hemisphere, such an expression does not refer to the same time interval and its normalization should be different. Of course, one may argue that it is the summer with respect to the local documents' creation time (if processing news-style documents) or with respect to a document's geographic scope (if processing narrative-style documents). But for processing heterogeneous document collections, one may want to be able to distinguish between normalized northern and southern summer (and general seasonal) references.

Furthermore, an expression such as *"winter 2003"* is even ambiguous if we assume the northern hemisphere. Does the expression refer to the beginning of 2003 or to the end of 2003? Of course, one point of view here is that the expression itself is vague and therefore should not be normalized more precisely than it is. But if the information is known, a temporal tagger should assign it to the expression.

FREE-TEXT TEMPORAL EXPRESSIONS

Finally, temporal information—in the sense of references to time points and durations—is available in a wide range of phrases. Throughout the book, we described and discussed temporal expressions as they are defined in annotation standards and specifications such as the temporal markup language TimeML. However, in addition to temporal expressions, many more phrases carry temporal information implicitly. For instance, references to named events or facts such as (i) *"the Battle of Gettysburg"*, (ii) *"the Champions League Final"*, and even (iii) *"Barack Obama's first term"* all refer to specific dates or time spans, namely (i) to July 1, 1863–July 3, 1863, (ii) to May 28, 2016 (assuming a reference to the final of the year 2016), and (iii) to January 20, 2009–January 19, 2013 (considering the dates of his inaugurations).

General phrases not covered by standard definitions of temporal expressions can be considered as free-text temporal expressions and can also be addressed by temporal taggers. This leads to a temporal enrichment of documents and to a better understanding of the content described in them. While first approaches toward comprehensive tagging of textual phrases with temporal scopes have recently been suggested [Kuzey et al., 2016a,b], assigning temporal scopes to free-text temporal expressions could be the next major task in the area of temporal information extraction. Applications in many areas that are exploiting temporal information could benefit from richer temporal information about documents.

Bibliography

David Ahn, Sisay Fissaha Adafre, and Maarten de Rijke. Towards task-based temporal extraction and recognition. In Graham Katz, James Pustejovsky, and Frank Schilder, Eds., *Annotating, Extracting and Reasoning about Time and Events*, number 05151 in Dagstuhl Seminar Proceedings, 2005. DOI: 10.1007/978-3-540-75989-8_1. 16

James Allan. Introduction to topic detection and tracking. In James Allan, Ed., *Topic Detection and Tracking: Event-based Information Organization*, chapter 1, pages 1–16. Kluwer Academic Publishers, Norwell, MA, 2002. 4

James F. Allen. Maintaining knowledge about temporal intervals. *Communications of the ACM*, 26(11), pages 832–843, 1983. DOI: 10.1145/182.358434. 11

Omar Alonso, Michael Gertz, and Ricardo Baeza-Yates. On the value of temporal information in information retrieval. *ACM SIGIR Forum*, 41(2), pages 35–41, 2007. DOI: 10.1145/1328964.1328968. 6, 15, 16

Omar Alonso, Jannik Strötgen, Ricardo Baeza-Yates, and Michael Gertz. Temporal information retrieval: Challenges and opportunities. In *Proc. of the 1st International Temporal Web Analytics Workshop (TWAW '11)*, pages 1–8. CEUR-WS.org, 2011. 6, 11, 25

Gabor Angeli and Jakob Uszkoreit. Language-independent discriminative parsing of temporal expressions. In *Proc. of the 51st Annual Meeting of the Association for Computational Linguistics (ACL '13)*, pages 83–92, 2013. 101, 103

Gabor Angeli, Christopher D. Manning, and Daniel Jurafsky. Parsing time: Learning to interpret time expressions. In *Proc. of the 2012 Conference of the North American Chapter of the Association for Computational Linguistics: Human Language Technologies (NAACL-HLT '12)*, pages 446–455, 2012. 101

Yoav Artzi and Luke Zettlemoyer. UW SPF: University of Washington Semantic Parsing Framework. Technical report, University of Washington, 2013. 95

Giuseppe Attardi, Valerio Basile, Cristina Bosco, Tommaso Caselli, Felice Dell'Orletta, Simonetta Montemagni, Viviana Patti, Maria Simi, and Rachele Sprugnoli. State of the art language technologies for Italian: The EVALITA 2014 perspective. *Intelligenza Artificiale*, 9(1), pages 43–61, 2015. DOI: 10.3233/ia-150076. 33

Saliha Azzam, Kevin Humphreys, and Robert J. Gaizauskas. Using coreference chains for text summarization. In *Proc. of the Workshop on Coreference and Its Applications (CorefApp '99)*, pages 77–84, ACL, 1999. DOI: 10.3115/1608810.1608825. 8

Krisztian Balog, Arjen P. de Vries, Pavel Serdyukov, and Ji-Rong Wen. The first international workshop on entity-oriented search (EOS). *ACM SIGIR Forum*, 45(2), pages 43–50, 2012. DOI: 10.1145/2093346.2093353. 7

Valentina Bartalesi Lenzi and Rachele Sprugnoli. Evalita 2007: Description and results of the TERN task. *Intelligenza Artificiale*, 4(2), pages 55–57, 2007. 33, 36, 40

Klaus Berberich, Srikanta J. Bedathur, Omar Alonso, and Gerhard Weikum. A language modeling approach for temporal information needs. In *Proc. of the 32nd European Conference on Advances in Information Retrieval (ECIR '10)*, pages 13–25, Springer, 2010. DOI: 10.1007/978-3-642-12275-0_5. 6, 16, 23, 24

Steven Bethard. A synchronous context free grammar for time normalization. In *Proc. of the 2013 Conference on Empirical Methods in Natural Language Processing (EMNLP '13)*, pages 821–826, ACL, 2013a. 101

Steven Bethard. ClearTK-TimeML: A minimalist approach to TempEval 2013. In *Proc. of the 7th International Workshop on Semantic Evaluation (SemEval '13)*, pages 10–14, ACL, 2013b. 95, 100, 101

Steven Bethard, Philip V. Ogren, and Lee Becker. ClearTK 2.0: Design patterns for machine learning in UIMA. In *Proc. of the 9th International Conference on Language Resources and Evaluation (LREC '14)*, pages 3289–3293, ELRA, 2014. 100

Steven Bethard, Leon Derczynski, Guergana Savova, James Pustejovsky, and Marc Verhagen. SemEval-2015 task 6: Clinical TempEval. In *Proc. of the 9th International Workshop on Semantic Evaluation (SemEval '15)*, pages 806–814, ACL, 2015. DOI: 10.18653/v1/s15-2136. 4, 34, 36, 52, 54, 65, 82

Douglas Biber. *Variation across Speech and Writing*. Cambridge University Press, Cambridge, UK, 1988. DOI: 10.1017/cbo9780511621024. 48

André Bittar, Pascal Amsili, Pascal Denis, and Laurence Danlos. French TimeBank: An ISO-TimeML annotated reference corpus. In *Proc. of the 49th Annual Meeting of the Association for Computational Linguistics (ACL '11)*, pages 130–134, 2011. 23, 41

Stephan Busemann, Thierry Declerck, Abdel K. Diagne, Luca Dini, Judith Klein, and Sven Schmeier. Natural language dialogue service for appointment scheduling agents. In *Proc. of the 5th Conference on Applied Natural Language Processing (ANLP '97)*, pages 25–32, ACL, 1997. DOI: 10.3115/974557.974563. 16

Ricardo Campos, Gaël Dias, Alípio M. Jorge, and Adam Jatowt. Survey of temporal information retrieval and related applications. *ACM Computing Surveys*, 47(2), pages 15:1–15:41, 2014. DOI: 10.1145/2619088. 6

Tommaso Caselli. It-TimeML: TimeML Annotation Scheme for Italian. Version 1.3.1. Technical report, Instituto di Linguistica Computazionale C.N.R., 2010. 23, 33

Tommaso Caselli, Valentina Bartalesi Lenzi, Rachele Sprugnoli, Emanuele Pianta, and Irina Prodanof. Annotating events, temporal expressions and relations in Italian: the It-TimeML experience for the Ita-TimeBank. In *Proc. of the 5th Linguistic Annotation Workshop (LAW '11)*, pages 143–151, ACL, 2011. 23, 40

Tommaso Caselli, Rachele Sprugnoli, Manuela Speranza, and Monica Monachini. EVENTI: EValuation of events and temporal INformation at Evalita 2014. In *Proc. of the 4th International Workshop EVALITA (EVALITA '14)*, pages 27–34, 2014. 21, 33, 36, 91

Angel X. Chang and Christopher D. Manning. SUTime: A library for recognizing and normalizing time expressions. In *Proc. of the 8th International Conference on Language Resources and Evaluation (LREC '12)*, pages 3735–3740, ELRA, 2012. 91, 92

Angel X. Chang and Christopher D. Manning. SUTime: Evaluation in TempEval-3. In *Proc. of the 7th International Workshop on Semantic Evaluation (SemEval '13)*, pages 78–82, ACL, 2013. 92, 99

Tao Chen and Min-Yen Kan. Creating a live, public short message service corpus: The NUS SMS corpus. *Language Resources and Evaluation*, 47(2), pages 299–335, 2013. DOI: 10.1007/s10579-012-9197-9. 51, 61

Nancy A. Chinchor. Overview of MUC-7/MET-2. In *Proc. of the 7th Message Understanding Conference (MUC-7)*, 1998. 19, 31

Nancy A. Chinchor and Patricia Robinson. MUC-7 named entity task definition (version 3.5). In *Proc. of the 7th Message Understanding Conference (MUC-7)*, 1998. 31

Francisco Costa and António Branco. TimeBankPT: A timeML annotated corpus of Portuguese. In *Proc. of the 8th International Conference on Language Resources and Evaluation (LREC '12)*, pages 3727–3734, ELRA, 2012. 23, 41

Leon Derczynski. Determining the types of temporal relations in discourse. Ph.D. thesis, University of Sheffield, 2013. 15

Leon Derczynski, Hector Llorens, and Estela Saquete. Massively increasing TIMEX3 resources: A transduction approach. In *Proc. of the 8th International Conference on Language Resources and Evaluation (LREC '12)*, pages 3754–3761, ELRA, 2012. 42, 50

Leon Derczynski, Jannik Strötgen, Ricardo Campos, and Omar Alonso. Time and information retrieval: Introduction to the special issue. *Information Processing and Management*, 51(6), pages 786–790, 2015. DOI: 10.1016/j.ipm.2015.05.002. 6

Leon Derczynski, Jannik Strötgen, Diana Maynard, Mark A. Greenwood, and Manuel Jung. GATE-Time: Extraction of temporal expressions and events. In *Proc. of the 10th International Conference on Language Resources and Evaluation (LREC '16)*, pages 3702–3708, ELRA, 2016. 91

Lisa Ferro, Inderjeet Mani, Beth Sundheim, and George Wilson. TIDES Temporal Annotation Guidelines—Version 1.0.2. Technical report, The MITRE Corporation, 2001. 19, 20

Lisa Ferro, Laurie Gerber, Janet Hitzeman, Elizabeth Lima, and Beth Sundheim. ACE Time Normalization (TERN) 2004 English Training Data v 1.0. Linguistic Data Consortium (LDC), Philadelphia, PA, 2005a. https://catalog.ldc.upenn.edu/LDC2005T07 [last accessed: May 15, 2016]. 37

Lisa Ferro, Laurie Gerber, Inderjeet Mani, Beth Sundheim, and George Wilson. TIDES 2005 Standard for the Annotation of Temporal Expressions. Technical report, The MITRE Corporation, 2005b. 19, 20

Lisa Ferro, Laurie Gerber, Inderjeet Mani, Beth Sundheim, and George Wilson. ACE Time Normalization (TERN) 2004 English Evaluation Data v 1.0. Linguistic Data Consortium (LDC), Philadelphia, PA, 2010. https://catalog.ldc.upenn.edu/LDC2010T18 [last accessed: May 15, 2016]. 37

Frank Fischer and Jannik Strötgen. When does German literature take place?—On the analysis of temporal expressions in large corpora. In *Proc. of the Digital Humanities Conference (DH '15)*, 2015. 68

Jonathan G. Fiscus and George R. Doddington. Topic detection and tracking evaluation overview. In James Allan, Ed., *Topic Detection and Tracking: Event-based Information Organization*, chapter 2, pages 17–32. Kluwer Academic Publishers, Norwell, MA, 2002. 4

Corina Forascu and Dan Tufis. Romanian TimeBank: An annotated parallel corpus for temporal information. In *Proc. of the 8th International Conference on Language Resources and Evaluation (LREC '12)*, pages 3762–3766, ELRA, 2012. 23, 41

Fredric Gey, Ray R. Larson, Noriko Kando, Jorge Machado, and Tetsuya Sakai. NTCIR-GeoTime overview: Evaluating geographic and temporal search. In *Proc. of the 8th NTCIR Workshop Meeting on Evaluation of Information Access Technologies*, pages 147–153, NII, 2010. 7

Fredric Gey, Ray R. Larson, Jorge Machado, and Masaharu Yoshioka. NTCIR9-GeoTime overview: Evaluating geographic and temporal search: round 2. In *Proc. of the 9th NTCIR Workshop Meeting on Evaluation of Information Access Technologies*, pages 9–17, NII, 2011. 7

Kevin Gimpel, Nathan Schneider, Brendan O'Connor, Dipanjan Das, Daniel Mills, Jacob Eisenstein, Michael Heilman, Dani Yogatama, Jeffrey Flanigan, and Noah A. Smith. Part-of-speech tagging for twitter: Annotation, features, and experiments. In *Proc. of the 49th Annual Meeting of the Association for Computational Linguistics (ACL '11)*, pages 42–47, 2011. 61

Ralph Grishman and Beth Sundheim. Design of the MUC-6 evaluation. In *Proc. of the 6th Message Understanding Conference (MUC-6)*, pages 1–11, 1995. DOI: 10.3115/1072399.1072401. 31, 36

Marta Guerrero Nieto and Roser Saurí. ModeS TimeBank 1.0. Linguistic Data Consortium (LDC), Philadelphia, PA, 2012. https://catalog.ldc.upenn.edu/LDC2012T01 [last accessed: May 15, 2016]. 41

Marta Guerrero Nieto, Roser Saurí, and Miguel A. Bernabe Poveda. ModeS TimeBank: A modern spanish TimeBank corpus (ModeS TimeBank: Un corpus TimeBank del español moderno). *Procesamiento del Lenguaje Natural*, 47(1), pages 259–267, 2011. 41

Kadri Hacioglu, Ying Chen, and Benjamin Douglas. Automatic time expression labeling for English and Chinese text. In *Proc. of the 6th International Conference on Intelligent Text Processing and Computational Linguistics (CICLing '05)*, pages 548–559, Springer, 2005. DOI: 10.1007/978-3-540-30586-6_59. 86, 88

Péter Halácsy, András Kornai, and Csaba Oravecz. HunPos: An open source trigram tagger. In *Proc. of the 45th Annual Meeting of the Association for Computational Linguistics (ACL '07)*, pages 209–212, 2007. DOI: 10.3115/1557769.1557830. 95

Erhard Hinrichs. Temporal anaphora in discourses of English. *Linguistics and Philosophy*, 9(1), pages 63–82, 1986. 15, 16

Daniel Jurafsky and James H. Martin. *Speech and Language Processing: An Introduction to Natural Language Processing, Computational Linguistics, and Speech Recognition*. Prentice Hall, Upper Saddle River, NJ, 2nd ed., 2008. 2, 15

Nattiya Kanhabua, Roi Blanco, and Kjetil Nørvåg. Temporal information retrieval. *Foundations and Trends in Information Retrieval*, 9(2), pages 91–208, 2015. 6

Oleksandr Kolomiyets and Marie-Francine Moens. Meeting TempEval-2: Shallow approach for temporal tagger. In *Proc. of the NAACL-HLT Workshop on Semantic Evaluations: Recent Achievements and Future Directions (SEW '09)*, pages 52–57, ACL, 2009. DOI: 10.3115/1621969.1621979. 37, 88

Oleksandr Kolomiyets and Marie-Francine Moens. KUL: Recognition and normalization of temporal expressions. In *Proc. of the 5th International Workshop on Semantic Evaluation (SemEval '10)*, pages 325–328, ACL, 2010. 88

Dilek Küçük and Dogan Küçük. On TimeML-Compliant temporal expression extraction in Turkish. *CoRR: The Computing Research Repository*, 2015. http://arxiv.org/abs/1509.00963 23

Erdal Kuzey and Gerhard Weikum. Extraction of temporal facts and events from wikipedia. In *Proc. of the 2nd Temporal Web Analytics Workshop (TempWeb '12)*, pages 25–32, ACM, 2012. DOI: 10.1145/2169095.2169101. 4

Erdal Kuzey, Vinay Setty, Jannik Strötgen, and Gerhard Weikum. As time goes by: Comprehensive tagging of textual phrases with temporal scopes. In *Proc. of the 25th International Conference on World Wide Web (WWW '16)*, pages 915–925, ACM, 2016a. 111

Erdal Kuzey, Jannik Strötgen, Vinay Setty, and Gerhard Weikum. Temponym tagging: Temporal scopes for textual phrases. In *Proc. of the 6th Temporal Web Analytics Workshop (TempWeb '16)*, pages 841–842, ACM, 2016b. 111

David Y. W. Lee. Genres, registers, text types, domains and styles: Clarifying the concepts and navigating a path through the BNC jungle. *Language Learning and Technology*, 5(3), pages 37–72, 2001. 48

Kenton Lee, Yoav Artzi, Jesse Dodge, and Luke Zettlemoyer. Context-dependent semantic parsing for time expressions. In *Proc. of the 52nd Annual Meeting of the Association for Computational Linguistics (ACL '14)*, pages 1437–1447, 2014. DOI: 10.3115/v1/p14-1135. 92, 97, 98

Johannes Leveling. Tagging of temporal expressions and geological features in scientific articles. In *Proc. of the 9th Workshop on Geographic Information Retrieval (GIR '15)*, pages 6:1–6:10, ACM, 2015. DOI: 10.1145/2837689.2837701. 109

Hui Li, Jannik Strötgen, Julian Zell, and Michael Gertz. Chinese temporal tagging with Heidel-Time. In *Proc. of the 14th Conference of the European Chapter of the Association for Computational Linguistics (EACL '14)*, pages 133–137, ACL, 2014. DOI: 10.3115/v1/e14-4026. 39, 103, 104

Xiaoyan Li and W. Bruce Croft. Time-based language models. In *Proc. of the 12th ACM International Conference on Information and Knowledge Management (CIKM '03)*, pages 469–475, ACM, 2003. DOI: 10.1145/956863.956951. 6

Hector Llorens, Estela Saquete, and Borja Navarro. TIPSem (English and Spanish): Evaluating CRFs and semantic roles in TempEval-2. In *Proc. of the 5th International Workshop on Semantic Evaluation (SemEval '10)*, pages 284–291, ACL, 2010. 89, 90

Hector Llorens, Leon Derczynski, Robert J. Gaizauskas, and Estela Saquete. TIMEN: An open temporal expression normalisation resource. In *Proc. of the 8th International Conference on Language Resources and Evaluation (LREC '12)*, pages 3044–3051, ELRA, 2012a. 50, 101

Hector Llorens, Naushad UzZaman, and James F. Allen. Merging temporal annotations. In *Proc. of the 19th International Symposium on Temporal Representation and Reasoning (TIME '12)*, pages 107–113, IEEE, 2012b. DOI: 10.1109/time.2012.14. 39

Hector Llorens, Nathanael Chambers, Naushad UzZaman, Nasrin Mostafazadeh, James F. Allen, and James Pustejovsky. SemEval-2015 task 5: QA TempEval—Evaluating temporal information understanding with question answering. In *Proc. of the 9th International Workshop on Semantic Evaluation (SemEval '15)*, pages 792–800, ACL, 2015. DOI: 10.18653/v1/s15-2134. 4, 8, 25, 34, 36

Bernardo Magnini, Emanuele Pianta, Christian Girardi, Matteo Negri, Lorenza Romano, Manuela Speranza, Valentina Bartalesi Lenzi, and Rachele Sprugnoli. I-CAB: The italian content annotation bank. In *Proc. of the 5th International Conference on Language Resources and Evaluation (LREC '06)*, pages 963–968, ELRA, 2006. 40

Juha Makkonen, Helena Ahonen-myka, and Marko Salmenkivi. Topic detection and tracking with spatio-temporal evidence. In *Proc. of the 25th European Conference on Advances in Information Retrieval (ECIR '03)*, pages 251–265, Springer, 2003. DOI: 10.1007/3-540-36618-0_18. 6

Giulio Manfredi, Jannik Strötgen, Julian Zell, and Michael Gertz. HeidelTime at EVENTI: Tuning Italian resources and addressing TimeML's empty tags. In *Proc. of the 4th International Workshop EVALITA (EVALITA '14)*, pages 39–43, 2014. 103

Inderjeet Mani and George Wilson. Robust temporal processing of news. In *Proc. of the 38th Annual Meeting of the Association for Computational Linguistics (ACL '00)*, pages 69–76, ACL, 2000a. DOI: 10.3115/1075218.1075228. 19, 88

Inderjeet Mani and George Wilson. Temporal granularity and temporal tagging of text. In *Proc. of the AAAI-2000 Workshop on Spatial and Temporal Granularity*, pages 71–73. AAAI, 2000b. 16

Christopher D. Manning and Hinrich Schütze. *Foundations of Statistical Natural Language Processing*. The MIT Press, Cambridge, MA, 6th ed., 2003. 25

Christopher D. Manning, Prabhakar Raghavan, and Hinrich Schütze. *Introduction to Information Retrieval*. Cambridge University Press, New York, NY, 2008. DOI: 10.1017/cbo9780511809071. 81

Elaine March and Dennis Perzanowski. MUC-7 evaluation of IE technology: Overview of result. In *Proc. of the 7th Message Understanding Conference (MUC-7)*, 1998. 36

Pawel Mazur. *Broad-coverage rule-based processing of temporal expressions*. Ph.D. thesis, Macquarie University and Wroclaw University of Technology, 2012. 16, 21, 31, 32, 35, 36, 53, 82, 86, 89

Pawel Mazur and Robert Dale. The DANTE temporal expression tagger. In *Proc. of the 3rd Language and Technology Conference (LTC '09)*, pages 245–257, Springer, 2009. DOI: 10.1007/978-3-642-04235-5_21. 89

Pawel Mazur and Robert Dale. WikiWars: A new corpus for research on temporal expressions. In *Proc. of the 2010 Conference on Empirical Methods in Natural Language Processing (EMNLP '10)*, pages 913–922, ACL, 2010. 49, 57, 61, 89

Pawel Mazur and Robert Dale. LTIMEX: Representing the local semantics of temporal expressions. In *Proc. of the Federated Conference on Computer Science and Information Systems (FedCSIS '11)*, pages 201–208, IEEE, 2011. 80

Donald Metzler, Rosie Jones, Fuchun Peng, and Ruiqiang Zhang. Improving search relevance for implicitly temporal queries. In *Proc. of the 32nd Annual International ACM SIGIR Conference on Research and Development in Information Retrieval (SIGIR '09)*, pages 700–701, ACM, 2009. DOI: 10.1145/1571941.1572085. 6

Anne-Lyse Minard, Manuela Speranza, Eneko Agirre, Itziar Aldabe, Marieke van Erp, Bernardo Magnini, German Rigau, and Ruben Urizar. SemEval-2015 task 4: TimeLine: Cross-document event ordering. In *Proc. of the 9th International Workshop on Semantic Evaluation (SemEval '15)*, pages 778–786, ACL, 2015. DOI: 10.18653/v1/s15-2132. 4

Anne-Lyse Minard, Manuela Speranza, Ruben Urizar, Begona Altuna, Marieke van Erp, Anneleen Schoen, and Chantal van Son. MEANTIME, the NewsReader multilingual event and time corpus. In *Proc. of the 10th International Conference on Language Resources and Evaluation (LREC '16)*, pages 4417–4422, ELRA, 2016. 21, 41

Paramita Mirza. Recognizing and normalizing temporal expressions in indonesian texts. In *Proc. of the 14th International Conference of the Pacific Association for Computational Linguistics (PACLING '15), Revised Selected Papers*, pages 135–147, Springer, 2015. DOI: 10.1007/978-981-10-0515-2_10. 42, 101

Paramita Mirza and Anne-Lyse Minard. FBK-HLT-time: A complete Italian temporal processing system for EVENTI-EVALITA 2014. In *Proc. of the 4th International Workshop EVALITA (EVALITA '14)*, pages 39–43, 2014. 101

Véronique Moriceau and Xavier Tannier. French resources for extraction and normalization of temporal expressions with HeidelTime. In *Proc. of the 9th International Conference on Language Resources and Evaluation (LREC '14)*, pages 3239–3243, ELRA, 2014. 103

David Nadeau and Satoshi Sekine. A survey of named entity recognition and classification. *Linguisticae Investigationes*, 30(1), pages 3–26, 2007. DOI: 10.1075/bct.19.03nad. 2

Matteo Negri and Luca Marseglia. Recognition and normalization of time expressions: ITC-irst at TERN 2004. Technical report, ITC-irst Trento, 2004. 88

Matteo Negri, Estela Saquete, Patricio Martínez-Barco, and Rafael Muñoz.   Evaluating knowledge-based approaches to the multilingual extension of a temporal expression normalizer. In *Proc. of the Workshop on Annotating and Reasoning about Time and Events (ARTE '06)*, pages 30–37, ACL, 2006. DOI: 10.3115/1629235.1629240. 103

Cam-Tu Nguyen, Xuan-Hieu Phan, and Thu-Trang Nguyen. JVnTextPro: A Java-based Vietnamese text processing tool. Version 2.0, 2010. http://jvntextpro.sourceforge.net/ [last accessed: May 15, 2016]. 95

Sérgio Nunes, Cristina Ribeiro, and Gabriel David. Use of temporal expressions in web search. In *Proc. of the 30th European Conference on Advances in Information Retrieval (ECIR '08)*, pages 580–584, Springer, 2008. DOI: 10.1007/978-3-540-78646-7_59. 6

Philip V. Ogren, Philipp G. Wetzler, and Steven Bethard. ClearTK: A UIMA toolkit for statistical natural language processing. In *Proc. of the Towards Enhanced Interoperability for Large HLT Systems: UIMA for NLP Workshop*, pages 32–38, 2008. 100

Siim Orasmaa. Towards an integration of syntactic and temporal annotations in estonian. In *Proc. of the 9th International Conference on Language Resources and Evaluation (LREC '14)*, pages 1259–1266, ELRA, 2014. 42

Marius Pasca. Towards temporal web search. In *Proc. of the 2008 ACM Symposium on Applied Computing (SAC '08)*, pages 1117–1121, ACM, 2008. DOI: 10.1145/1363686.1363946. 7

Octavian Popescu and Carlo Strapparava. SemEval 2015, task 7: Diachronic text evaluation. In *Proc. of the 9th International Workshop on Semantic Evaluation (SemEval '15)*, pages 870–878, ACL, 2015. DOI: 10.18653/v1/s15-2147. 4

James Pustejovsky, José M. Castaño, Robert Ingria, Roser Saurí, Robert J. Gaizauskas, Andrea Setzer, Graham Katz, and Dragomir R. Radev. TimeML: Robust specification of event and temporal expressions in text. In *Proc. of the New Directions in Question Answering Symposium (NDQA '03)*, pages 28–34, AAAI, 2003a. 15, 19, 20

James Pustejovsky, Patrick Hanks, Roser Saurí, Andrew See, Robert J. Gaizauskas, Andrea Setzer, Dragomir R. Radev, Beth Sundheim, David Day, Lisa Ferro, and Marcia Lazo. The TIMEBANK corpus. In *Proc. of Corpus Linguistics 2003*, pages 647–656, UCREL, 2003b. 38

James Pustejovsky, Robert Knippen, Jessica Littman, and Roser Saurí. Temporal and event information in natural language text. *Language Resources and Evaluation*, 39(2), pages 123–164, 2005. DOI: 10.1007/s10579-005-7882-7. 8, 19, 20, 22

James Pustejovsky, Kiyong Lee, Harry Bunt, and Laurent Romary. ISO-TimeML: An international standard for semantic annotation. In *Proc. of the 7th International Conference on Language Resources and Evaluation (LREC '10)*, pages 394–397, ELRA, 2010. 19, 20

Nitin Ramrakhiyani and Prasenjit Majumder. Approaches to temporal expression recognition in Hindi. *ACM Transactions on Asian and Low-resource Language Information Processing*, 14(1), pages 2:1–2:22, 2015. DOI: 10.1145/2629574. 42

Alan Ritter, Sam Clark, Mausam, and Oren Etzioni. Named entity recognition in tweets: An experimental study. In *Proc. of the 2011 Conference on Empirical Methods in Natural Language Processing (EMNLP '11)*, pages 1524–1534, ACL, 2011. 61

Estela Saquete. ID 392: TERSEO + T2T3 transducer. A systems for recognizing and normalizing TIMEX3. In *Proc. of the 5th International Workshop on Semantic Evaluation (SemEval '10)*, pages 317–320, ACL, 2010. 22

Estela Saquete and James Pustejovsky. Automatic transformation from TIDES to TimeML annotation. *Language Resources and Evaluation*, 45(4), pages 495–523, 2011. DOI: 10.1007/s10579-011-9147-y. 22, 42

Estela Saquete, Patricio Martínez-Barco, and Rafael Muñoz. Automatic multilinguality for time expression resolution. In *Proc. of the 3rd Mexican International Conference on Artificial Intelligence (MICAI '04)*, pages 458–467, IEEE, 2004. DOI: 10.1007/978-3-540-24694-7_47. 103

Estela Saquete, Rafael Muñoz, and Patricio Martínez-Barco. Event ordering using TERSEO system. *Data and Knowledge Engineering*, 58(1), pages 70–89, 2006. DOI: 10.1016/j.datak.2005.05.011. 88

Roser Saurí and Toni Badia. Spanish TimeBank 1.0. Linguistic Data Consortium (LDC), Philadelphia, PA, 2012a. https://catalog.ldc.upenn.edu/LDC2012T12 [last accessed: May 15, 2016]. 23, 40

Roser Saurí and Toni Badia. Catalan TimeBank 1.0: Corpus Documentation. Technical report, Barcelona Media, 2012b. 42

Roser Saurí, Estela Saquete, and James Pustejovsky. Annotating time expressions in Spanish. TimeML Annotation Guidelines. Technical report BM 2010-02, Barcelona Media, 2010. 23

Frank Schilder and Christopher Habel. From temporal expressions to temporal information: Semantic tagging of news messages. In *Proc. of the ACL-2001 Workshop on Temporal and Spatial Information Processing (TASIP '01)*, pages 65–72, ACL, 2001. DOI: 10.3115/1118238.1118247. 15, 16

Helmut Schmid. Probabilistic part-of-speech tagging using decision trees. In *Proc. of the International Conference on New Methods in Language Processing*, pages 44–49, 1994. 95

Sadi Evren Seker and Banu Diri. TimeML and Turkish temporal logic. In *Proc. of the 2010 International Conference on Artificial Intelligence (ICAI' 10)*, pages 881–887, CSREA Press, 2010. 23

Christian Sengstock and Michael Gertz. CONQUER: A system for efficient context-aware query suggestions. In *Proc. of the 20th International Conference on World Wide Web (WWW '11)*, pages 265–268, ACM, 2011. DOI: 10.1145/1963192.1963305. 6

Andrea Setzer and Robert J. Gaizauskas. Annotating events and temporal information in newswire texts. In *Proc. of the 2nd International Conference on Language Resources and Evaluation (LREC '00)*, pages 1287–1294, ELRA, 2000. 19

Milad Shokouhi and Kira Radinsky. Time-sensitive query auto-completion. In *Proc. of the 35th Annual International ACM SIGIR Conference on Research and Development in Information Retrieval (SIGIR '12)*, pages 601–610, ACM, 2012. DOI: 10.1145/2348283.2348364. 6

Luka Skukan, Goran Glavaš, and Jan Šnajder. HeidelTime.Hr: Extracting and normalizing temporal expressions in croatian. In *Proc. of the 9th Language Technologies Conference (LTC '14)*, pages 99–103, 2014. 23, 49, 50, 103, 104

Carlota S. Smith. The syntax and interpretation of temporal expressions in English. *Linguistics and Philosophy*, 2(1), pages 43–99, 1978. DOI: 10.1007/bf00365130. 16

Kathrin Spreyer and Anette Frank. Projection-based acquisition of a temporal labeller. In *Proc. of the 3rd International Joint Conference on Natural Language Processing (IJCNLP '08)*, pages 489–496, ACL, 2008. 103

Josef Steinberger, Massimo Poesio, Mijail A. Kabadjov, and Karel Jeek. Two uses of anaphora resolution in summarization. *Information Processing and Management*, 43(6), pages 1663–1680, 2007. DOI: 10.1016/j.ipm.2007.01.010. 8

Jannik Strötgen. *Domain-sensitive temporal tagging for event-centric information retrieval*. Ph.D. thesis, Heidelberg University, 2015. 14, 48

Jannik Strötgen and Michael Gertz. HeidelTime: High quality rule-based extraction and normalization of temporal expressions. In *Proc. of the 5th International Workshop on Semantic Evaluation (SemEval '10)*, pages 321–324, ACL, 2010. 90, 91

Jannik Strötgen and Michael Gertz. WikiWarsDE: A German corpus of narratives annotated with temporal expressions. In *Proc. of the Conference of the German Society for Computational Linguistics and Language Technology (GSCL '11)*, pages 129–134, 2011. 49, 90, 103

Jannik Strötgen and Michael Gertz. Event-centric search and exploration in document collections. In *Proc. of the 12th ACM/IEEE Joint Conference on Digital Libraries (JCDL '12)*, pages 223–232, ACM, 2012a. DOI: 10.1145/2232817.2232859. 3, 6

Jannik Strötgen and Michael Gertz. Temporal tagging on different domains: Challenges, strategies, and gold standards. In *Proc. of the 8th International Conference on Language Resources and Evaluation (LREC '12)*, pages 3746–3753, ELRA, 2012b. 51, 53, 61, 64, 72, 82, 90

Jannik Strötgen and Michael Gertz. Multilingual and cross-domain temporal tagging. *Language Resources and Evaluation*, 47(2), pages 269–298, 2013. DOI: 10.1007/s10579-012-9179-y. 90, 91, 103

Jannik Strötgen and Michael Gertz. A baseline temporal tagger for all languages. In *Proc. of the 2015 Conference on Empirical Methods in Natural Language Processing (EMNLP '15)*, pages 541–547, ACL, 2015. DOI: 10.18653/v1/d15-1063. 90, 104, 105, 108

Jannik Strötgen, Michael Gertz, and Pavel Popov. Extraction and exploration of spatio-temporal information in documents. In *Proc. of the 6th Workshop on Geographic Information Retrieval (GIR '10)*, pages 16:1–16:8, ACM, 2010. DOI: 10.1145/1722080.1722101. 90

Jannik Strötgen, Julian Zell, and Michael Gertz. HeidelTime: Tuning English and developing spanish resources for TempEval-3. In *Proc. of the 7th International Workshop on Semantic Evaluation (SemEval '13)*, pages 15–19, ACL, 2013. 95, 103

Jannik Strötgen, Ayser Armiti, Tran Van Canh, Julian Zell, and Michael Gertz. Time for more languages: Temporal tagging of Arabic, Italian, Spanish, and Vietnamese. *ACM Transactions on Asian Language Information Processing*, 13(1), pages 1:1–1:21, 2014a. DOI: 10.1145/2540989. 23, 37, 49, 50, 103, 104

Jannik Strötgen, Thomas Bögel, Julian Zell, Ayser Armiti, Tran Van Canh, and Michael Gertz. Extending HeidelTime for temporal expressions referring to historic dates. In *Proc. of the 9th International Conference on Language Resources and Evaluation (LREC '14)*, pages 2390–2397, ELRA, 2014b. 51, 59, 97

William Styler, Steven Bethard, Sean Finan, Martha Palmer, Sameer Pradhan, Piet C. de Groen, Brad Erickson, Timothy Miller, Chen Lin, Guergana Savova, and James Pustejovsky. Temporal annotation in the clinical domain. *Transactions of the Association for Computational Linguistics*, 2, pages 143–154, 2014a. 34, 52, 53

William Styler, Guergana Savova, Martha Palmer, James Pustejovsky, Tim O'Gorman, and Piet C. de Groen. THYME annotation guidelines. Technical report, 2014b. 34

Bernhard Suhm, Lori Levin, Noah Coccaro, Jamie Carbonell, Ryosuke Isotani, Alon Lavie, Laura Mayfield, Carolyn P. Rosé, Carol Van Ess-Dykema, and Alex Waibel. Speech-language integration in a multi-lingual speech translation system. In *Proc. of the Workshop on Integration of Natural Language and Speech Processing*, AAAI, 1994. 50

Weiyi Sun, Anna Rumshisky, Ozlem Uzuner, Peter Szolovits, and James Pustejovsky. 2012 i2b2 Temporal relations challenge annotation guidelines. Technical report, 2012. 33

Weiyi Sun, Anna Rumshisky, and Ozlem Uzuner. Evaluating temporal relations in clinical text: 2012 i2b2 challenge. *Journal of the American Medical Informatics Association*, 20(5), pages 806–813, 2013a. DOI: 10.1136/amiajnl-2013-001628. 33, 36, 52

Weiyi Sun, Anna Rumshisky, and Ozlem Uzuner. Annotating temporal information in clinical narratives. *Journal of Biomedical Informatics*, 46, pages S5–S12, 2013b. DOI: 10.1016/j.jbi.2013.07.004. 52

Xavier Tannier. Extracting news web page creation time with DCTFinder. In *Proc. of the 9th International Conference on Language Resources and Evaluation (LREC '14)*, pages 2037–2042, ELRA, 2014. 71, 102, 103

Hegler Tissot, Angus Roberts, Leon Derczynski, Genevieve Gorrell, and Marcos Didonet Del Fabro. Analysis of temporal expressions annotated in clinical notes. In *Proc. of the 11th Joint ACL-ISO Workshop on Interoperable Semantic Annotation (ISA '15)*, pages 93–102, ACL, 2015. 52

Kristina Toutanova, Dan Klein, Christopher D. Manning, and Yoram Singer. Feature-rich part-of-speech tagging with a cyclic dependency network. In *Proc. of the Human Language Technology Conference of the North American Chapter of the Association for Computational Linguistics (HLT-NAACL '03)*, pages 173–180, ACL, 2003. DOI: 10.3115/1073445.1073478. 95

Naushad UzZaman, Hector Llorens, Leon Derczynski, James F. Allen, Marc Verhagen, and James Pustejovsky. SemEval-2013 task 1: TempEval-3: Evaluating time expressions, events, and temporal relations. In *Proc. of the 7th International Workshop on Semantic Evaluation (SemEval '13)*, pages 1–9, ACL, 2013. 4, 21, 25, 27, 29, 32, 36, 38, 39, 87, 91, 92, 95, 96, 101

Matje van de Camp and Henning Christiansen. Resolving relative time expressions in dutch text with constraint handling rules. In *Proc. of the 7th International Workshop on Constraint Solving and Language Processing (CSLP '12)*, pages 74–85, Springer, 2012. DOI: 10.1007/978-3-642-41578-4_10. 103

Marc Verhagen. Tempeval2 Data—Release Notes. Brandeis University, 2011. `http://timeml.org/site/timebank/tempeval/tempeval2-data.zip` [last accessed: November 9, 2015]. 39

Marc Verhagen and Jessica Moszkowicz. AQUAINT TimeML 1.0 Corpus Documentation. Brandeis University, 2008. `http://www.timeml.org/site/timebank/aquaint-timeml/aquaint_timeml_1.0.tar.gz` [last accessed: November 9, 2015]. 38

Marc Verhagen and James Pustejovsky. Temporal processing with the TARSQI toolkit. In *Proc. of the 22nd International Conference on Computational Linguistics (COLING '08)*, pages 189–192, ACL, 2008. 88

Marc Verhagen and James Pustejovsky. The TARSQI toolkit. In *Proc. of the 8th International Conference on Language Resources and Evaluation (LREC '12)*, pages 2043–2048, ELRA, 2012. 88

Marc Verhagen, Inderjeet Mani, Roser Saurí, Robert Knippen, Seok Bae Jang, Jessica Littman, Anna Rumshisky, Jon Phillips, and James Pustejovsky. Automating temporal annotation with TARSQI. In *Proc. of the 43rd Annual Meeting of the Association for Computational Linguistics (ACL '05)*, pages 81–84, 2005. DOI: 10.3115/1225753.1225774. 88

Marc Verhagen, Robert J. Gaizauskas, Frank Schilder, Mark Hepple, Graham Katz, and James Pustejovsky. SemEval-2007 task 15: TempEval temporal relation identification. In *Proc. of the 4th International Workshop on Semantic Evaluation (SemEval '07)*, pages 75–80, ACL, 2007. DOI: 10.3115/1621474.1621488. 4, 32

Marc Verhagen, Robert J. Gaizauskas, Frank Schilder, Mark Hepple, Jessica Moszkowicz, and James Pustejovsky. The TempEval challenge: Identifying temporal relations in text. *Language Resources and Evaluation*, 43(2), pages 161–179, 2009. DOI: 10.1007/s10579-009-9086-z. 2, 32

Marc Verhagen, Roser Saurí, Tommaso Caselli, and James Pustejovsky. SemEval-2010 task 13: TempEval-2. In *Proc. of the 5th International Workshop on Semantic Evaluation (SemEval '10)*, pages 57–62, ACL, 2010. 4, 29, 32, 36, 38, 90, 91

Christopher Walker, Stephanie Strassel, Julie Medero, and Kazuaki Maeda. ACE 2005 Multilingual Training Corpus. Linguistic Data Consortium (LDC), Philadelphia, PA, 2006. https://catalog.ldc.upenn.edu/LDC2006T06 [last accessed: May 15, 2016]. 37

Ruiqiang Zhang, Yuki Konda, Anlei Dong, Pranam Kolari, Yi Chang, and Zhaohui Zheng. Learning recurrent event queries for web search. In *Proc. of the 2010 Conference on Empirical Methods in Natural Language Processing (EMNLP '10)*, pages 1129–1139, ACL, 2010. 6

Authors' Biographies

JANNIK STRÖTGEN

Jannik Strötgen is a postdoctoral researcher at the Max Planck Institute for Informatics in Saarbrücken, Germany. He studied computational linguistics and economics at Heidelberg University, Germany and received his Magister Artium in 2009. Between 2009 and 2015, he worked as a research assistant at the Computer Science department in Heidelberg. In March 2015, he defended his Ph.D. thesis, in which he worked on temporal, geographic, and event-centric information extraction and retrieval supervised by Prof. Dr. Michael Gertz. In the context of his thesis, the domain-sensitive and multilingual temporal tagger HeidelTime has been developed. It was made publicly available and is constantly improved. For more details, please see:

    http://people.mpi-inf.mpg.de/~jstroetge/

MICHAEL GERTZ

Michael Gertz is a full professor at Heidelberg University where he heads the database systems group at the faculty of Mathematics and Computer Science. He received his diploma in Computer Science from the University of Dortmund, Germany, and his Ph.D. from the University of Hanover, Germany, in 1996. From 1997 until 2008 he was on the faculty at the University of California at Davis. He currently serves on the editorial board of the *ACM Transactions on Spatial Algorithms and Systems*, and he is an associate editor of the *ACM Journal on Data and Information Quality*. His research interests include the management and analysis of temporal, spatial, and spatio-temporal data, data mining, text mining, and social network analysis. For more details, please see:

    http://dbs.ifi.uni-heidelberg.de/

Index

Printed in the United States
by Baker & Taylor Publisher Services